Language and the Sexes

Language
and
the Sexes

Francine   Frank
       and
Frank   Anshen

State University of New York Press
ALBANY

Published by
State University of New York Press, Albany

For information, address State University of New York Press, State University
Plaza, Albany, N.Y., 12246

Library of Congress Cataloging in Publication Data

Frank, Francine Harriet Wattman, 1931-
    Language and the sexes.

    Bibliography: p.
    Includes index.
    1. English language—United States—Sex differences.
2. Sexism in language. 3. Women—United States—Language.
4. Men—United States—Language. 5. Sex role. I. Anshen,
Frank, 1942-   II. Title.
PE2808.F73   1984   420'.1'9   83-24141
ISBN 0-87395-881-0
ISBN 0-87395-882-9 (pbk.)

10 9 8 7 6 5 4 3 2 1

Contents

To our most loyal friends and supporters,
our families

Preface

When faced with yet another book clamoring for her attention, the harried reader has a right to ask, why this book and why these authors? The focal point of this book is an examination of the many ways in which language both reflects and influences the roles and status of women and men in our society. The authors believe that such an examination will be useful to those who want to understand the structure of our society as well as those who want to change it.

Our collaboration on this book grew out of our mutual interest in the relationship of language to sexual equality. By profession and avocation we are linguists. We recognize the central role of language in human culture and society. Both of us have taught courses in sociolinguistics in which we have dealt with the subject of language and the sexes; we have also written independently on the topic, and have read much of the sizeable and growing body of literature in the field. Our teaching and reading convinced us that the expansion and increasing specialization of research activity had created the need for a book such as this one—one which would present the important issues from the perspective of linguistics and still be accessible to the general public, one which would also raise linguistic consciousness about the social implications of language and linguistic usage. Rashly, perhaps, we set out to write such a book.

Although this volume is not specifically intended as a textbook, we hope that teachers of English, Women's

1

Studies, and Linguistics may find it appropriate for their students. For their convenience, we have appended a list of projects and suggestions for research. We have also yielded a bit to the temptation of advocacy and included a brief set of guidelines for non-sexist language usage.

Many people have helped in the preparation of this book. We acknowledge first of all our debt to the many researchers whose cumulative efforts form the basis of our discussion, and especially those who shared with us their unpublished research. The names of some, but by no means all, of these people are found in our bibliography. In addition, friends, family, and colleagues have read all or part of the manuscript and offered valuable comments and suggestions. We list below the names of a few who have been of special help: Mary Ann Rafferty and Lauren De Sole read the entire manuscript and provided us with their reactions as students; Martha Schultz gave us valuable suggestions from the perspective of a secondary school teacher; Miriam Isaacs, John Holm, and Billie Anshen all read at least one draft and provided encouragement and advice. Fran Kelly typed our first draft with speed and efficiency and contributed valuable editorial advice; Carol Tansey, our illustrator, also supplied both typing and editorial assistance; and Bertha Wakin provided word-processing help in producing the guidelines.

Finally, we must thank one another. While writing this book, we learned a great deal about our subject and about the process of collaboration. We argued over many details, we encouraged one another at difficult moments, and we took up the challenge of reconciling two very different writing styles. Our shared goals saw us through and we produced a true collaboration—we cannot say "this chapter is yours and that one is mine,"—the credit is equally shared and so must be the responsibility for any errors or shortcomings which remain.

Introduction

This book is about language and the sexes, how women and men use language, how society uses language to favor one sex over the other, and how we can analyze language to reveal society's disparate views and treatment of the sexes. Why should we examine language if we are interested in the problem of sexism in our society? Why not concentrate instead on questions of inequity in the legal system or employment practices? We will answer this question by showing that language is a crucial element in these and other aspects of our lives; in fact, it is probably the single most important characteristic of human beings.

Language is universal among humans in two respects. First, all human cultures have language. Explorers braving the jungles of the Amazon, the deserts of Arabia, or the halls of Congress have yet to find a group of humans who do not have language. Furthermore, none of these languages are primitive in the sense that they lack the potential of expressing ideas which can be expressed in other of the world's languages. Thus, all human species have languages which are equally useful in formulating ideas.

The second way in which language is universal is that it is used by virtually all members of a society. While making axes, or leading religious services, or programming computers may involve skills possessed by only a small group in any given culture, nearly everybody over the age of three or so talks, sometimes incessantly. If a child does not follow this pattern, parents will become very

3

concerned. And rightly so, as humans who cannot speak have serious mental, physical, or emotional problems. Moreover, it should be pointed out that many of those who cannot speak or hear because of physical disabilities are not without language; in the deaf community in the United States, American Sign Language fills the role taken by English among the hearing and provides further evidence of the universality of language among humans.

Finally, we find that human language is limited to humans. Neither dolphins, nor bees, nor chimpanzees in their natural state have anything which is close to human language. When chimpanzees such as Washoe, Sarah, and Lana are taught to use language, they become much more human-like to us. Whether these chimpanzees actually have learned a human-like language is a question we leave for others to resolve. We might note here• that extra-terrestrial beings invented by science fiction writers usually are endowed with a language or some superior form of communication evolved from language.

Human society as we know it, or as our ancestors for several millenia knew it, would be impossible without speech. Language allows humans to cooperate in large-scale, complex patterns. It further allows these patterns to be modified; both the patterns and the modifications may then be passed on to future generations as a base on which they can build. Technology, architecture, law, mathematics, and religion are only a few of the human constructs which could exist only at the most rudimentary levels, if at all, without language. Writing, a relatively recent invention in the history of the human race, has extended our abilities to preserve and transmit knowledge and experience and has become almost as important as speech in modern technological societies.

The importance of language seems to be recognized in all human societies. In our own, the biblical story of creation mentions a linguistic act, the naming of the animals, as the first act performed by a human. The Bible also cites an act of linguistic retrogression, the mixing of the languages at

Babel, as a decisive event, which both punished presumptuous humans and widened the gap between humanity and God. At another level, magic spells and obscene words reflect our belief that language can directly affect the physical world. The power is in the words themselves, not in their referents; the words of a spell must be repeated exactly, synonyms are not allowed. Similarly, the embarrassment involved in speaking about sex and excrement is much mitigated if we use terms with a Latin origin and avoid "four-letter" Anglo-Saxon words. To the best of our knowledge, no child has ever faced having her or his mouth washed out with soap for saying *copulate* or *excrement*.

Another sign of the importance which people in our society attribute to language can be seen in the school system. A great amount of time and effort which might be alternatively used is invested in teaching children to use the language "correctly," that is, in accordance with certain received ideas of proper usage. We are taught to admire and aspire to "good grammar," we devote an enormous amount of time to learning a sadistic spelling system, and we are instructed to look to "the dictionary" as the authority on the correct form and use of words. We also learn to judge people by the way they speak and to mistrust people who do not use the language in the prescribed ways. Members of minority groups may learn to imitate the language of those who hold power, while those who belong to the dominant group may learn to dislike and disparage the language of some minorities. Although the teaching of such attitudes is implicit in the way society regards language and is not often explicitly stated, the effects are no less real.

People do not often consider what a language reveals about a society's customs and beliefs about the world. For many of us, an attempt to learn a foreign language brings the first realization that other people may view the world differently from the way we do, that they may categorize and talk about experience in quite different ways. Those who are fortunate enough to be bilingual may already know this, but to most of us it can be quite a shock. We may find it peculiar that some languages have more than one word for *you* or even *we*, or that in many languages all nouns must belong to one of the classes labelled masculine, or feminine, or neuter. We find it difficult to understand why, in certain languages, we have to express *I like spaghetti* as *Spaghetti is pleasing to me*. Or why, in other languages, there is a perverse insistence on having separate words for *father's brother* and *mother's brother* when it is perfectly clear that they are both uncles. When we learn that these societies also assign different responsibilities towards a child to maternal and paternal uncles, the logic in having separate terms becomes clear. The experience of learning a second language which categorizes the world differently is excellent preparation for examining the assumptions about the world embedded in our own language and linguistic usages.

Our use of language also reflects the prejudices of our society in more subtle ways. Again, we are often unaware of this and we go on speaking "naturally" until someone brings it to our attention. The civil rights movement made many people conscious of the ways in which the English language reflects negative stereotypes about Blacks and other minority groups. The existence of the verb *to welsh* tells us a great deal about the attitudes of the English to the people they displaced, and the verb *to gyp* probably reflects negative stereotypes about the people who call themselves Rom. Afro-Americans are certainly not comforted by such English expressions as *blackguard* and *black marks*, and the many other instances where the term *black* has a negative connotation. More recently, the women's movement has focused attention on the sexist elements in our language and in the way we use it. We discover that, in many respects, standard English is a language which reflects the values of white middle-class males. As our linguistic consciousness is raised and we become aware of the many negative words for women, as well as for members of different ethnic groups, we may feel that it is appropriate to try to avoid such terms. Our discomfort with the words, however, does not necessarily mean that we have changed the social attitudes which gave rise to them, only that we are more conscious of such attitudes. We may also become aware that our ways of addressing people often reflect the relative status and power of one group vis-à-vis another. This is evident in the practice of using first names more readily for women, while using titles such as *Mr.* and *Dr.* more often for men. We may begin to recognize the stereotypes involved in referring to *nurses* and *male nurses* in one breath, and to *doctors* and *women doctors*, or even *lady doctors*, in the next. We may wonder about the origin and effect of the use of *man* and *he* sometimes to refer to males only, and at other times to include women as well as men. We may or may not think it desirable or possible to change these practices, but we are becoming increasingly aware of their existence and potential social significance. Feminists have also made us conscious of our stereotyped ideas about the way women and men speak, and have posed such questions as whether women really do nag and gossip and, in general, talk more than do men.

The remainder of this book will explore some of the ways in which our language mirrors the sexism in our society. We hope to encourage the reader to think about how we all may unconsciously be perpetuating sexism and other prejudices through our unquestioning use of our native language, even though we consciously reject these prejudices. The topics we will discuss include the importance of names, our knowledge and beliefs about the differences between the speech of women and men, how men and women talk to one another, and how we use language to talk about the sexes. Finally, we will look at some of the changes occurring today and our participation in these changes as individuals and as members of a social group. Throughout the book we will raise many questions and call on our readers to observe and become more conscious of their own linguistic usage and the language of others. We hope to encourage the formulation of answers and the raising of other, equally important, questions.

1

Naming Names

> "What's in a name? That which we call a rose by any other name would smell as sweet."
>
> Shakespeare, *Romeo and Juliet*

What's in a name? Linguists tell us that names are only arbitrary sequences of sounds that the speakers of a language use to label the world around them. Whether we call it *equus* or *ma, caballo* or *at, Pferd* or *horse* does not change the nature of the four-legged animal to which these labels apply: the choice of labels merely indicates that we are speaking Latin or Chinese, Spanish or Turkish, German or English. Obviously, if we want to communicate with speakers of a particular language, we must choose the label appropriate to that language. It would not do to say *horse* when speaking to a Chinese, any more than it would be helpful to use the word *ma* when speaking to an American. However, the appropriateness of the label is dependent upon the particular language, and is in no way determined by the nature of horses. Shakespeare, of course, expressed this view more poetically.

We may accept the reasoning of the linguists, but as a group we do not act as if we believe them. In fact, the overwhelming majority of people act as if the name of something (an object or person) were an inherent part of its nature, and as if changing the name might alter the object or person in some significant way. We seem to echo

Gertrude Stein and reply to Shakespeare that a "rose is a rose is a rose is a rose." When we admire a strange flower or tree, we immediately want to know what it is called. "That's a gingko," someone says, and we feel content; we now have a label and we "know" the tree. Similarly, when the young son of one of the authors would eat nothing but strained cauliflower for two weeks, his parents were comforted by the pediatrician's announcement that the child was undergoing a "food fad." To return to our tree, if nobody can help us out with a name, we may examine the leaves and the configuration of the branches carefully and actually acquire some detailed knowledge of the tree, but we do not feel we "know" it without its name. If we cannot find the name, we are permitted to invent one, but first we usually exhaust all possibilities to discover an existing, and therefore "correct," name. Thus, the European colonists in North America took the names of many localities, plants and animals from the native inhabitants, who presumably knew the correct names.

On those occasions when we truly have to invent a new name, we resort to various strategies to do so: we may attach a person's name to a new object, as in *Rubik's Cube*, or we may convert a proper name into a label for something new, as in *bloomers*, named for Amelia J. Bloomer, a nineteenth century feminist and social reformer; alternatively, we may try to remember some Latin or Greek and come up with terms like *television* or *video*, or with parts of words, as in the second half of *speedometer*; we may create an acronym like *NATO* or *snafu*. On the other hand, if we are naming some new commercial product, it might be well to consider the economic advantages of following the modern tendency to create a name with at least one "x"—*Kleenex, Exxon, Kotex, Memorex,* and *Xerox* being but a few examples.

Names are important to all human societies, and in many they are viewed as a source of power for good or evil ends. It is not difficult to understand how this belief in the power of names developed. Language, as we pointed out in the introductory chapter of this book, defines humanity;

naming is, in turn, the most obvious and basic function of language. If names are a property of the named, the right of naming brings with it the power to define the named. The Bible provides us with many examples of the importance of naming. According to the Book of Genesis, the first human act is the naming of the animals. Through this act, humans gain dominion over the animals. The relationship between humans and animals is fixed: humans have language, animals don't; humans name animals, animals don't name humans; humans have dominion over animals, the reverse is not true. The power which comes from the right to name is indeed awesome. How powerful then, must God's name be! Such is its power that one of the Ten Commandments was devoted to regulating its use and Orthodox Jews are one of the groups which will not utter it. There is said to be a group of Buddhist monks in Tibet compiling all of the names of God; when they are finished, the world is to end.

Again and again we find in the Bible that when events of great religious significance occur, the people involved must take new names to accommodate their new religious role. When Abram enters into a covenant with God, thus founding the Jewish people, he becomes Abraham, and his wife Sarai becomes Sarah. In the New Testament, after Saul becomes a Christian, he is known as Paul. The change of names to express religious change continues today in our own society, in many contexts. American Blacks who embrace Islam often take new names to symbolize their new identity. The most famous case is probably that of the former heavy-weight boxing champion who chose to be called Muhammed Ali rather than Cassius Clay. Other prominent examples include Malcolm X and Kareem Abdul-Jabbar. In a like manner, Roman Catholics often add a name when they are confirmed, and it is common practice for those who enter a religious order to take a new name. Among Jews, it is traditional to have a separate Hebrew name for religious purposes.

The importance of naming others and controlling one's own name is by no means limited to religious contexts, nor to Western societies. Naming is a consequential act in every human culture we know. In some societies, names are believed to be so special that one guards one's name from strangers, who might be able to do you harm if they knew your name. In other societies, names are subject to taboos, with certain persons being prohibited from using the names of other individuals. Thus, an Apache man may not utter the name of his mother-in-law. The power to control one's own name is emphasized in some American Indian cultures, where young people are not given names, but are sent out to discover their real names. Again, in our own society, philosophers and students of symbolic logic spend an enormous amount of time worrying about the nature of names. Those interested in a further discussion of the nature of names are referred to Lewis Carroll's *Through the Looking Glass*, where the White Knight explains to Alice that the name of the song he wishes to sing is "The Aged, Aged Man," although the song is called "Ways and Means." The name of the song is called "Haddocks' Eyes," but, of course, the song is "A-sitting on a Gate."

In our own culture, we find parents-to-be agonizing and often arguing over prospective names for their children, while children and adults agonize over appropriate names for their pets or even their cars. Most of us have strong feelings about our given names, ranging from pride to acceptance to dislike and rejection; we may try to take control over them by adopting nicknames or completely different names. Psychologically, given names seem to have a real effect on children's self-image and behavior. Joans raise different expectations than do Lisas, and we expect different things from Bobs than from Percys. And, in the same vein as a change of name to signify religious change, we find people changing their names to reflect a change in political beliefs. Thus, Patricia Hearst asserted her political rebirth by taking the new name Tanya, and later marked her return to her former values by reclaiming her old name. Some newspaper commentators reacted to this by talking about Patricia Hearst and Tanya as if they really were two different people. People who have very disparate parts to their lives may even take two different names: Charles Dodgson did mathematics while Lewis Carroll wrote children's stories. Writers, in particular, seem to find it desirable to create a new name to use for their authorial selves. Mark Twain, George Sand, George Orwell, and Saki are just a few of the examples which spring to mind. Actors, of course, also commonly adopt new names for stage and screen, and these pseudonyms frequently become their "real" names for the general public.

During the sixties and seventies, many Blacks adopted African names as an affirmation of their ethnic origin. Similarly, many feminists have taken new names as a political statement. Some of the first names they have chosen, such as *Jade* or *Star*, evoke an identification with nature, folklore, even with witchcraft; the last names they have adopted often reflect a rejection of patriarchal naming practices. As we might expect from what has been said earlier in this chapter, the matter of changing one's name is not always treated lightly by society. Once the political statement involved is recognized, there often follows an attempt by society to reject the political stance by rejecting the name change. Not incidentally, this rejection may also be seen as an attempt to retain the naming power for society. Thus, the transformation of Cassius Clay into Muhammed Ali caused a great deal of controversy, none of which concerned the structure or aesthetics of the two phonetic sequences. Later in this chapter, we will discuss some examples of resistance to women's claims of power over their own names.

We conclude that, despite the scientific validity of the linguists' view, names are not indifferent labels, but have very real social significance for all human cultures. It is therefore not surprising to find that in our own society, women and men are treated very differently when it comes to naming customs, and that these differences often reflect with great clarity the sexism of our society.

The most prominent difference between women's and men's names in American society is the transitory nature of a woman's last name. Traditionally, this serves to identify her in terms of her relation to the men in her life. She starts out life with her father's name, which she trades for her husband's last name if she marries. If her husband dies, she retains his name, and she may even keep it after a divorce. Should she remarry, she may get yet another replacement. Our modern practice is a direct continuation of earlier customs. Before people began using surnames, about the thirteenth century in English society, married women were labelled by their husband's given name. In medieval England, we might find reference to Johanna Jackwyf, or to Syssat, wife of Thomas the cook. An extensive discussion of these and other naming practices is found in Una Stannard's book *Mrs. Man.*

Women's traditional name changing provides additional evidence that a change of names is not an inconsequential act; women have had little or no say in the matter and therefore, both the custom and the involuntary way it operates reflect the status of women in our society. Although it may be an exaggeration to say that these naming practices label women as the property of the men whose names they are assigned, they certainly reflect the dominance of one sex in the family. A judge in a Midwestern state has recently ruled that a man has a legally enforceable right to have his children bear his last name and their mother, even if she has custody of the children, cannot have them bear her own last name without showing in court that the need to change overcomes the father's presumptive rights.

One might argue that, ideally, it is appropriate for a couple to express the unity of their marriage by choosing to share a name, but it does not seem ideal that the shared name is always the husband's. One of the consequences of this practice is that continuity of names is accorded almost exclusively to males. Where there are no sons to preserve the family name, we speak of the family "dying out," regardless of the number of daughters and their children. Most of us know our mother's maiden name, but that knowledge is restricted enough that banks use it as a check on identification; few of us remember our grandmothers' maiden names, and even fewer know those of our great-grandmothers.

For a woman in today's world, the constant changeability of her name is a nuisance at the very least; driver's licenses, social security cards, school records, and credit documents all have to be changed. A woman who works and has established a professional reputation finds that adopting her husband's name may actually set her back in her field. An established writer or researcher, for example, may suddenly become a "newcomer" and unrecognizable if her work begins to appear under a new name. Because of this, many professional women either continue to use their father's name in professional contexts, or hyphenate their old name with the new one. Indeed, we find a minor tradition turning into a significant trend, as women increasingly refuse to wander through life taking one man's name after another. One alternative was adopted by the nineteenth century feminist, Lucy Stone, who, upon her marriage to Henry Blackwell in 1855, chose to retain her own name, a decision which caused considerable controversy at that time and since.

The custom of calling women by their husband's first name as well as his last name, as in Mrs. John Jones, did not become common in this country until the nineteenth century. It was first used by women of the upper class and was long considered a sign of snobbishness. Most married women were known by a name such as Mrs. Ann Jones. When the new custom did catch on, it spread so rapidly that the refusal of feminist Elizabeth Cady Stanton in the 1840's to be known as Mrs. Henry B. Stanton was viewed as a conscious revolutionary stand, which set feminists apart from non-feminists.

In recent years, a growing number of women have chosen to follow Lucy Stone's example, while others have decided to discard their father's name and create their own. These personal decisions have had interesting repercussions. It is, of course, possible to go to court to obtain judicial recognition of a name change, but it has not been necessary. English Common Law, which is followed in this country, has traditionally left the choice, spelling, and pronunciation of personal names almost entirely to the discretion of the individual concerned, as long as there is no intent to defraud. So, Norma Jean Baker had no trouble calling herself Marilyn Monroe. Likewise, the traditional adoption of pseudonyms by certain groups of professionals has encountered few problems, and many immigrants have "Americanized" their names as part of the process of assimilation. This "Americanization" has not always been a voluntary act; the great-grandfather of one of the authors, a Mr. Bogoslavsky, was somewhat surprised on leaving Ellis Island to discover that he was now Mr. Davis. Such cases represented an assertion of the power to name by the dominant segment of society.

However, when significant numbers of women began to exercise the traditional right to control their own names, many found the way blocked by bureaucratic and judicial hurdles. Some women who chose not to take their husband's name were, with the approval of the Supreme Court, denied the right to register to vote or obtain a driver's license using any but their husband's last name; others found banks unwilling or uncooperative in matters involving mortgages and joint accounts. The state of Hawaii even went so far as to pass a law, since repealed, requiring women to use their husband's last name.

Similarly, women who wish to change their names for feminist purposes have also run into problems. A few years ago, Ellen Cooperman, a woman living on Long Island, was refused permission by a judge to change her last name to Cooperperson on the grounds that it would be harmful to the women's movement. Clearly, the judge's refusal to allow a woman to choose her own name furthers the women's movement, although this consequence was probably not exactly what the judge had in mind. In contrast to the obstacles encountered by some women who have attempted to assert their right to keep or alter their own names, the path is clear for those who prefer to follow tradition and adopt their husband's name. Usually, no documentation is required, and driver's license applications and the like often state that, for a name change by reason of marriage, all one has to do is fill in a form.

Beyond the official pressure, many women find themselves spending an inordinate amount of time explaining to family and friends why they have chosen to defy custom in this way. It is perhaps surprising to find such hostility facing women who are seeking to exercise what has traditionally been every person's right, and which does no apparent harm to anybody. But women who choose to determine their names after marriage are explicitly questioning our culture's traditional concept of women's role in marriage. When one recalls the general importance of naming, it is no longer surprising that those who value the status quo resist the threats posed by women naming themselves in violation of long-standing practices. In much the same way, generations of boxers have used special names in the ring with no reaction or even notice by sportswriters, but Muhammed Ali's choice of a new name for religious purposes, especially for a controversial religion, inspired countless sportswriters to fly to the attack. In both cases, what appears to be a personal matter has moved into the public and political domain.

We should note that the resistance to women retaining their own names after marriage is greater than that to men changing their names for religious purposes. For some years after Cassius Clay became Muhammed Ali, certain sportswriters insisted on using the name Cassius Clay, but in time they got tired, and today, the use of the name Muhammed Ali is universal. By the time Lew Alcindor chose the name Kareem Abdul-Jabbar, the change was simply accepted with little or no fuss by sportswriters. On the other hand, many people feel they should call a woman by her "married" name even if she has declared that she does not have one. Thus, the *New York Times* and many other newspapers staunchly refuse to abide by women's choices as to what their own names should be. Nancy Lopez, the golfer, made clear her desire to continue to be Nancy Lopez professionally after her marriage. The *Times*, in its majesty, referred to her as Mrs. Melton until she got a divorce, presumably not merely to spite the *Times*.

As another alternative to the married woman's choice between her birth name and her husband's name, some couples adopt a combined hyphenated name. We also find some women, single and married, adopting their mother's birth name. Other trends include: fashioning a new name based upon maternal descent, such as Joan Mary's Daughter; desexing one's former name, as in Ellen Cooperperson, mentioned above; or creating an entirely new name, Varda One, for example. While these strategies may not threaten the institution of marriage, they do implicitly threaten male ownership and dominance of last names. Viewed in this light, the action of the Long Island judge in forbidding Ellen Cooperperson to name herself ceases to be merely ridiculous and can be seen as an attempt to maintain the status quo against serious attack.

Before leaving the subject of last names, we might consider the ways in which some other societies treat the matter. In Spanish-speaking countries, a woman retains her own name when she marries, adding her husband's name to it; if Margarita Sánchez marries Antonio Castillo, she is known as Margarita Sánchez de Castillo. Children also retain their mother's name, and the daughter of Margarita Sánchez might be Julia Castillo Sánchez. Before applauding this Hispanic practice, which appears less sexist than our own, we should note that the preposition *de* in Spanish commonly indicates possession. Also, if Julia marries, her maternal last name will probably be dropped in favor of her husband's name. Consequently, Julia's children will not bear the name Sánchez. The result is that the woman's surname lasts a couple of generations, but continuity of a name can still only occur through the male line. We might also note that in some Spanish-speaking countries, the custom of children using double last names which include their mother's name is losing ground in favor of "brevity." You can probably guess which name is sacrificed.

In Russia, naming customs provide two names in addition to a given name. The first is a patronymic, a name based on the father's first name. Russian is a language with grammatical gender; that is, there is a system of classification of all nouns that includes having different endings for words referring to men and women; consequently, the patronymics differ slightly between the sexes. Following the patronymic, there is a surname or family name, which is traditionally derived from a patronymic. These surnames also have different endings for women and men. In a family where Ivan is a favorite name, a young man might be called Ivan Ivanovich Ivanov while his sister might be Anna Ivanovna Ivanova. The use of these three names plus nicknames derived from them, accounts for much of the problem English speakers have keeping track of the characters in Russian novels. In another Slavic country, Bulgaria, the last element, the surname, remains. However, unlike the practice in Russia, a Bulgarian woman has a choice of surnames when she marries; she may keep her father's name or adopt her husband's surname. Of course, her mother's own surname is lost, no matter which alternative she selects.

Some countries are taking legal steps to assure women control of their names. The Swedish parliament, as reported in the October 1982 issue of *Ms.* magazine (p. 11), has ruled that married women and men may choose to be called by their own or their spouse's name. Parents will be able to choose the last name they wish their children to have, but if they do not do so within three months of the child's birth, the child will automatically receive the mother's last name.

First names, perhaps even more than last names, reflect the traditional sex-role standards of our society. There are few unisex names in America, and most of us automatically use first names to sort the unknown persons behind the names according to sex. Occasionally, a traditional man's name begins to be used for women; the most likely consequence is a sharp decline in its use as a name for boys. Sex-indifferent Francis/Frances and, more recently, Lee, are not uncommon, but nowadays one rarely meets a male Shirley, Beverly, Evelyn, or Gale (in any spelling). We might note that this Gresham's Law of Names does not seem to operate as strictly in the Confederacy, where Bobbies and Billies of both sexes are common. Some of the dual sex names, such as Shirley, Leslie, and Sidney, began as surnames which were bestowed on sons as given names in an attempt to assure family continuity. We see here that, as in the case of last names, it is the males who are counted on for continuity. Men's names are used as a source of women's first names in another way, one which allows men to keep their names "untainted" and reflects the subordinate position of women. Frequently, girls are given names which are feminizations of boys' names: Roberta, Charlotte, Francine, Henrietta. Many of these names are diminutives; as stated by Casey Miller and Kate Swift in their book *Words and Women*, "They are copies, not originals, and like so many other words applied to women, they can be diminishing" (p. 5).

An interesting fact about first names in this country is that almost all men's names function only as personal names, while many women bear names which also refer to some object or abstract quality. So, women may be named after virtues: Faith, Hope, Charity, Patience, Prudence, Chastity; or vegetation: Rose, Daisy, Iris, Heather, Olive, Myrtle, Flora; or calender units: April, May, June, Spring; or minerals: Pearl, Beryl, Ruby, Amber. Other western cultures follow similar patterns, but are more flexible in this respect, and we may find a man named Prudencio in the Hispanic world, or a Giacinto (Hyacinth) in Italy. In traditionally Catholic countries, children are named after saints and, although there are many female versions of the male names, boys are not usually named after female saints. An exception is Mary: Maria may form the second part of a male compound name such as Juan María or Giammaria in the Romance languages. In English, Marion, now a rather uncommon name for men, is also derived from Mary.

Although most of us are unaware of it, in English there are even characteristic differences in the sounds of women's and men's names. In an unpublished study of three hundred common names, one hundred and fifty women's names and one hundred and fifty men's names, Carol Larm found a number of phonetic differences between the two sets. These included the sounds most commonly spelled 'p', 't', 'k,' 'b', 'd', and 'g', sounds which phoneticians call "stops" because they are made by briefly stopping the flow of air from the lungs. While thirty percent of the men's names ended in one of these stops, only four percent of the women's names did. (Frank, Robert, Edward, Mike, Richard, are a few of the men's names; Pat, Peg, and names ending in -*ette* are most of the women's names.) One might speculate that terminating a name with a stop is perceived as too brusque to be "feminine," an idea which is supported when we find that fifty-four percent of the women's names studied ended in a vowel, but only fourteen percent of the men's names did so. More evidence that we like to linger over women's names comes from the fact that they tend to be longer: thirty percent of the men's names, but only twelve percent of the women's names, have only one syllable, while twenty-one percent of the women's names have three or more syllables, and only four percent of the men's names are this long. Part of the explanation for this lies in the fact, discussed earlier, that many women's names are derived from men's names by adding one or more syllables. In the study referred to, several women's names were formed this way (Christiana, Glenda, Jacqueline, Patricia, Paula, Roberta, and Stephanie). One can add many other women's names to this list, but there are no examples, in English, of the reverse process. This confirms once again that names of

men are viewed as primary and those of women as
secondary, a direct reflection of the traditionally dominant
position of men in our society.

Even when it comes to nicknames, men and women are
treated differently in American society. There are two
major ways nicknames are formed in English. One is
phonetically motivated from the actual name, usually the
first name, but occasionally, in cases like Mac MacDonald
and Tommy Thomson, from the last. The other major
method for forming nicknames is to refer to some attribute
of the named: Shorty, Lefty, Curly. This second type is
predominantly male, Sissy from sister being a common
exception, while the first type is more evenly distributed
across the sexes. However, as we might expect from the
transient nature of their last names, women rarely get
nicknames based on them. Macs are almost universally
male. If we examine in more detail those nicknames
phonetically derived from first names, we see that there are
in fact several major processes and numerous minor ones.
The single most frequent device is: cut the first name to its
first syllable and then either do or do not add -ie
(sometimes spelled -y). Accordingly, we have Al from
Alan, Jan from Janet, Marty from Martin, and both Sue
and Susie from Susan. It is interesting to note that this -ie
ending is frequently used in baby talk, and although it is
attached to nicknames for both sexes, it appears to have a
special affinity for female names. So, we can derive Pat as a
nickname for both Patrick and Patricia, but Patty is
almost always female, except in Irish-American usage,
where it is spelled "Paddy." Similarly, Fran and Chris are
used for both sexes, while Franny and Chrissie are only
female, at least after childhood. Somewhat similarly, we
get Al from Alan but Ellie from Ellen. A subgroup which
adds -sy (or -cy) is exclusively female: Betsy, Patsy, Elsie,
Francie, and Maisie, and the similar Babs.

Another process forms a nickname from a second or
third syllable, so we have Gail from Abigail or Bert from
Albert, Herbert, Colbert, or Hubert. Again, this process is

predominantly female. Holly Newell, in an unpublished paper on names, found twenty-nine examples from feminine names and only seven from masculine ones. Men, on the other hand, seem to have a near monopoly on one syllable nicknames starting with a vowel, such as Abe, Ed, and Art, although *Wizard of Oz* fans will remember Dorothy's Aunt Em. Men also own those nicknames formed by inserting a final -*k;* Rick, Hank, Chuck, and Frank (from Francis).

We can conclude, then, that naming practices for women and men in American society differ in many respects, and that, whether we are dealing with given names or family names, men generally take precedence over women. As Shakespeare knew, a rose may be a rose, but it makes a great difference whether one is a Montague or a Capulet.

2

Talking Like
a Lady:
How Women Talk

Consider the following claim: Women and men don't speak the same. Admittedly, in the United States of America, most people speak English. But they speak it differently, and the differences between women's and men's speech go beyond the variations in regional speech which we call dialects. Everybody knows that men and women *sound* different when they speak. Women have high-pitched voices which we may sometimes find to be shrill. They speak rapidly and often sound "emotional." Men, on the other hand, have deep, resonant voices; they speak more slowly than women. It is true that children of both sexes sound more or less alike, but when boys' voices change at puberty, the differences become clearcut. In matters of usage, women's speech tends to be more polite and more "grammatical" than that of men.

If the above description has a familiar ring, that is because it represents some of our traditional notions of sex differences in language behavior. But, we may ask, do men and women really speak different varieties of American English, as people from New York City and Texas speak different regional dialects? Are there systematic differences in pronunciation, vocabulary, and grammar between females and males that we can call "genderlects"? In this chapter, we will examine some of the common beliefs on this subject and attempt to determine whether they correspond to reality.

Before we begin our investigation of sex differences in American English, we might ask whether there are any cultures where men and women can truly be said to speak different languages. You may have noticed that the claims about our own language which we have echoed in the introductory paragraph are mostly relative, and generally include the word *more*. Women's speech is more polite, or more emotional, etc. We find, however, that for some languages, the differences are much sharper; women's speech has certain characteristics that men's speech does not have, and vice versa. This type of difference is called "sex-exclusive." For the Yana Indians of California, for example, many words used by men are longer than the same words used by women (Sapir 1929). In Koasati, a Muskogean language spoken in Louisiana, words that end in an 'l' or 'n' sound when spoken by women, end in an 's' sound when pronounced by men. To say "lift it" for example, a man would say *lakawhos,* while a woman would say *lakawhol* (Haas 1944). Among the Carib Indians, men and women were reported by early explorers to have different words for many common items, as if there were a different dictionary for male and female use. This was, apparently, caused by the fact that the native Arawaks had been conquered by Caribs, who killed the men and kept the women as slaves or wives. The women kept their native language and taught it to their children, thus making it the native language of succeeding generations. Upon reaching puberty, boys would learn the men's language, i.e. Carib. Actually, the Carib they learned was a pidginized Carib, since, as already noted, there were no native speakers of Carib after the first, conquering, generation. Although the sexual differences in vocabulary have largely been leveled, even today there are still a number of words which are considered more appropriate for men than women. (Holm 1978, pp. 384-8). (For further discussion of sex differences in various languages, see Bodine 1975b.)

One of the most intriguing cases of linguistic differentiation between the sexes is reported for Chiquita, a language native to Bolivia. The women do not classify nouns according to gender, but men make a formal distinction between two noun classes, using one for men and supernatural beings, and the other for all other nouns, including those that refer to women. Men maintain the distinction when speaking to other men, but, when men speak to women, they drop this use of gender or noun classes. It is tempting to speculate that women simply refuse to put up with this demonstration of male egotism.

Although some of the above differences may seem puzzling and exotic to us, we should remember that the societies where these languages are spoken are usually organized on the basis of an extensive and clearcut division of labor between women and men, and that, as a result, adults spend much of their time among people of the same sex. Under such circumstances, the development of specialized vocabulary is seen to be quite normal. Some of the other differences, such as variations in pronunciation, can be traced to the fact that the language is undergoing change in certain respects, and one sex is behaving more conservatively by preserving the older pronunciation. This should not surprise us, as all languages show signs of change, with some groups clinging to older forms and others preferring innovation. In contemporary English, for instance, women are usually linguistic innovators, adopting new pronunciations about a generation before men do. Although such behavior may be deliberate, as in the replacement of one word by another, it is more often unconscious.

English does not exhibit the sort of sex-exclusive linguistic variation described above, but speakers of English, as noted at the beginning of this chapter, do have a number of beliefs about ways in which women and men differ linguistically. These beliefs are strong enough and common enough to be labelled stereotypes. Upon closer examination, we find that these stereotypes have a complex and often confusing relationship to the truth.

Perhaps the most common stereotype about women's speech is that women talk a lot. If we take "a lot" to mean more than men, we are faced with the surprising fact that there seems to be no study which supports this belief, while there are several which show just the opposite. One such study, by Otto Sonder, Jr., is particularly interesting. Sonder organized discussion groups which included women and men and assigned them specific topics. The discussions were recorded and transcribed, but in the transcripts, the participants were identified only by letters, as A, B, etc. Panels of judges who tried to identify the sex of each speaker from these transcripts were correct about fifty-five percent of the time, a result which is better than chance, but not overwhelmingly so. Closer examination of the data, however, reveals some interesting facts. A word count of the recorded discussions showed a clear tendency for the men who participated in the study to utter more words than the women. In other words, men, on the average, actually talked more than did women. Even more interesting is the fact that individuals of either sex who talked a lot were more likely to be judged as males, while taciturn individuals of either sex were more likely to be identified as females. Not only does this study suggest that men are more talkative, it also suggests that the judges "knew" this fact and used it to make judgments about the sexual identity of unknown speakers. Although, consciously, they would probably subscribe to the cultural stereotype of the talkative woman, their judgments show that they knew that the real situation is the direct opposite of the stereotype.

How can we reconcile this apparent contradiction between our beliefs and our actions? It seems that people have an incorrect conscious stereotype of how much women and men talk, while at the same time having, at a less conscious level, the knowledge that men tend to speak more than women. When called upon to make judgments, they use their knowledge of actual behavior rather than the stereotype of presumed behavior. We are reminded of individuals in pre-Civil War America who thought slaves were lazy, in spite of the fact that they observed them doing backbreaking work from sunup to sundown.

Students of stereotypes believe that our preconceived notions influence our expectations and responses during initial contacts with strangers. However, when we get to know people even slightly, we usually treat them as individuals and ignore the stereotypes. This is commonly recognized as the "Some of my best friends are..." syndrome. We may, for example, believe that girls are, in general, more social than boys, even though that may not be true of our own children or, indeed, of any children we know well; or we may believe that women are more talkative than men, although members of our family or circle of friends do not act that way.

In an attempt to trace the development of the sort of stereotypes we have been discussing, Carole Edelsky investigated beliefs about women's and men's speech and how they are acquired by American children. She found that adults are often able to identify and discuss these stereotyped views, but may personally disclaim belief in them. Sometimes, however, the stereotypes may be so strong that they blind people to actual behavior which conflicts with them, especially their own behavior. For example, one man in Edelsky's study claimed that men would not use the expression *Oh dear* "because it's a protected word, more passive, that men don't use." About ten minutes later, this same man said: "I can't come up with anything. Oh dear, I'm just going to run the tape down" (p. 237). At one point in her study, the experimenter had trouble with the recorder when she was preparing to interview some children, and exclaimed, "Damn it, I can't get this thing plugged in." Later, many of the older children in the group responded negatively when asked "Do women ever say 'Damn it'?" The children's stereotyped view that "men swear, but ladies don't" evidently had more impact on them than what they had heard with their own ears (p. 243).

The reactions reported by Edelsky serve as reminders that people seem, in general, to be rotten observers of both their own and other people's linguistic behavior. They are astounded when they hear themselves on a tape recorder, not only because of the different voice quality, but also because they find their own pronunciation, sentence structure, and choice of words to be different from what they had thought. In extreme cases, an individual can write best-selling books telling the public to eschew usages that the author uses in everyday speech. Besides recording this ability of people to not believe their own ears, Edelsky demonstrates the pervasive nature of stereotypes of sex differences in language. The first-graders in her study have already developed stereotypes of how women and men speak and, by the time the children are in the sixth grade, they seem to agree entirely with adults on stereotypes of female and male speech.

There are many other common stereotypes about women's speech. Have you ever heard the one about the woman who told her husband to stop talking while she was interrupting? This sexist joke reflects a widely held stereotype that women interrupt in conversations more than do men. But it doesn't seem to reflect the facts. When Candace West and Don Zimmerman studied conversations, they found that ten of the eleven conversations between men and women contained interruptions but that, oddly enough, of the total of forty-eight interruptions, forty-six were by men. In other words, men interrupted women twenty-three times as often as women interrupted men. In contrast, only three of the twenty same-sex conversations showed any interruptions at all. What is going on here? Perhaps these results are not really so odd when we consider that interrupting is a violation of an individual's right to speak and is therefore often the privilege of the more powerful, while being interrupted is the fate of the less powerful. Perhaps, as it is news when woman bites dog, it is just this rarity of occurrence of women interrupting men which makes it so noticeable when it does happen. Then again, we may just be indulging our penchant for believing evil of women. Have you heard the one about the man who told his wife not to talk while he was interrupting?

Some interesting facts about how men exercise the prerogatives of male power in conversations between couples are revealed in a study by Pamela Fishman. She points out that conversation is "a process of ongoing negotiated activity between people" (p. 11). In order to have a conversation, the participants must interact on a number of levels and so we might well expect conversations between men and women to reflect the relative power of the sexes in our society. Firstly, to note the obvious, conversations must be about something, they must have a topic. Fishman analyzes how topics are initiated and controlled. In some twelve hours of recordings of spontaneous talk, seventy-six topics were raised, forty-seven by women and twenty-nine by men. But more than half, twenty-eight to be exact, of the women's topics failed; that is, although women brought up the topics, they did not become the subject of conversation. In contrast, all but one of the men's topics were successful, even though several of these were identical to a woman's topic which had failed. As a result of all this, of the forty-five successful topics, twenty-eight were proposed by men and only seventeen were proposed by women (p. 15).

Topic failure in Fishman's study was caused by the failure of the men to respond. Many women who work or live with men have had the experience of raising a topic or making a suggestion to a group composed mainly of men and receiving absolutely no response, only to find some time later, that when one of the men raises the same idea, it is greeted with interest and respect. How is one to react to such a situation? In the face of the failure of their conversation topics, women in Fishman's study resorted to a number of strategies, including the use of questions— women asked three times as many questions as men. Some people have claimed that women's frequent use of questions reflects a lack of assertiveness and self-confidence. Fishman points out that women may often use question forms because questions demand a response from the other person, thus assuring that the topic will continue at least a little while longer, even if it turns out to be just long enough to permit the male conversational partner to utter a grunt.

Other strategies employed by the women in Fishman's study included the expressions *D'y know what?* and *This is really interesting.* The first functions as an attention-getter and is often used by children to claim a right to speak. The natural response—*what?*—is an invitation to continue the conversational exchange. The second strategy *(this is really interesting),* used as an introductory remark, represents an attempt by the woman to establish interest in the topic on her own, as she cannot assume male cooperation. Finally, women used the expression *You know* ten times more frequently than did the men. Use of this form increased as men's responses decreased. Obviously, such expressions are not exclusive to women; men use them too, although they seem to need them much less, as women tend to support men's conversational topics. Women, then, are found to do much of the work in developing and sustaining these conversations, while men exercise veto power, picking and choosing among the topics offered by women for their approval. Women consistently help develop topics introduced by men, but much of the time, men respond to women's topics by silence or by minimal responses such as *uhm, hmh, mm,* etc. And this seems to be the way men want things, as who wouldn't, if they could get away with it? In *The New Seventeen Book of Etiquette and Young Living,* published in 1970, we find a "survey of opinions" of boys, who are reported to have said "I hate girls who can't stop talking," and "I like girls who listen to me without interrupting" (pp. 101–2). Apparently, such boys live in a world they enjoy.

The last three sets of findings which we have discussed: that men talk more than women do, that they interrupt more than women do, and that men determine the topics of conversation, are not unrelated; they have in common the fact that men are exercising superior power vis-à-vis women in conversation. Men get to talk more, at times of their own choosing, about topics which interest them. Conversations, then, seem to represent in microcosm the distribution of power in other areas of our lives. It is tempting to speculate that the superior scores which women, as a group, exhibit on standardized tests of verbal ability, represent the results of Darwinian evolution. Women need superior verbal skills just to get a word in edgewise!

One interesting fact that emerges from the preceding discussion of conversations is that silence is as important as speech in maintaining men's dominance in linguistic interactions. Men use silence to control conversations, then reduce women to silence by interrupting when they are speaking; similar behavior does not seem to occur when women speak to one another. Such observations have led some to refer to women as a "muted group," left only with the more "trivial" domain of private language, while the public use of language has been appropriated by men. In her discussion of the muted group approach, Cheris Kramarae recounts that "Some of the women in the early slavery abolition movement in the United States were encouraged to use in their writing rhetorical principles set up entirely by male British and American orators, and to sit silent on the platform while male ministers and relatives read the women's public address" (p. 29). Apparently, the first of these American women to speak publicly was a Black woman, Frances Maria W. Stewart. She gave a number of talks in Boston against slavery in 1832-33, then stopped, saying, "I have made myself contemptible in the eyes of many" (Oliver 1965, p. 439, cited by Eble 1975a, p. 6). Only four years earlier, on July 4, 1828, Frances Wright, a Scottish immigrant, had given the first public speech on record in this country as being delivered by a woman, an event regarded as scandalous at the time.

Stereotypes are curious things. As we have seen, they often do not correspond to reality. In addition, they have differing relations to our notions of ideal or desirable behavior. So we find that the stereotypical woman talks too much, while the ideal, for men at least, is "girls who listen." Clearly, the stereotypical woman falls far short of the ideal girl. On the other hand, we believe that women are more polite than men, do not curse or use obscenities, and use "better grammar." Politeness, avoidance of dirty words, and good grammar are, presumably, desirable traits in our culture. Perhaps we have here, finally, a stereotype which is advantageous to women and perhaps also, even one which is true. Is it not possible that women's speech is more proper than that of men? In this respect, it seems that our beliefs do coincide with the findings of linguists. Women appear to use forms which are considered to be correct more often than do men of similar age, education, social class, and region. One of the best studies showing this phenomenon was done by John Fischer in 1958. He investigated the pronunciation of words ending in -*ing* by elementary school children in a town in New England. As you know, these words have both a "proper" pronunciation and an "improper" one, in which they sound as if they end with -*in*. Most of the children used both pronunciations, as many of us do, but the girls used proportionately more of the "proper" forms, while the boys used more of the -*in* ones.

A number of other studies have found the same general tendency of women to use more "proper" language than men. Frank Anshen, for example, found that adult Black women in a North Carolina town were more likely to use standard pronunciation of words like *running, this,* and *mouth,* while men in the same town were more likely to pronounce these words *runnin', dis,* and *mouf.* One possible explanation for this "correctness" of women's speech is that they tend to be more status conscious than men in our society. Women are often judged on the basis of their social status and their adherence to prescriptive social norms; accordingly, they are socialized to exhibit "better" social behavior than men.

Peter Trudgill reports that women in Great Britain exhibit similar behavior to their American sisters. In Norwich, England, women used more "proper" language than did men. As for the men, they not only used more non-standard forms than did the women, but seemed to be unconsciously proud of the fact, reporting their speech to be even more non-standard than it was. The men were aware of the more standard forms and often stated that women speak "better," but they made no attempt to change their own speech to these better varieties. How do we explain this? Trudgill concludes that male speakers in general seem, subconsciously, to favor non-standard, low-status speech forms associated with the working class. Such speech has connotations of "toughness" and "masculinity" which gives it a sort of covert prestige. Similarly, William Labov found that New Yorkers' ratings of how well a male speaker would do in a fight went up as his use of standard forms declined. As further evidence, consider the recurrent theme in Western movies of the Eastern "dude" who ventures west, where everybody considers him a "sissy" because of his fancy clothes and speech. Usually, he beats up a gang of bad guys in the last reel, and the townspeople realize that he is a "real man," despite his speaking proper English. We have even borrowed terms from Spanish to describe such masculine oriented behavior. The expressions *macho* and *machismo* are not to be found in a 1952 dictionary, but they are accorded separate entries in a 1982 dictionary. We note, however, that *Webster's Ninth New Collegiate Dictionary* (Merriam-Webster, 1983, p. 714) dates *macho* from 1928 and *machismo* from 1947.

It seems, then, that there exist two kinds of prestige, the normally accepted one, which has more influence on women, and a covert prestige which has more influence on men. The full story may be more complex, however. Patricia Nichols has pointed out in her recent work that, although women's greater use of standard prestige features has generally been regarded as conservative linguistic behavior, in pronunciation and in some grammatical features, women have been found to be more innovative. She attributes the apparent paradox in part to a faulty system of categorizing women according to social class.

The traditional methods of sociology, adopted for many sociolinguistic studies, which classify a woman according to the social class of her husband or father, have been challenged as not reflecting the realities of modern society. So it may be that the findings regarding the linguistic behavior of women from certain social classes are also open to question.

Another point made by Nichols is that language prestige must be defined in terms of the immediate speech community. From this perspective, behavior such as women's more frequent use of -ing as opposed to -in may be innovative for speakers of a non-standard variety of English, but conservative for standard speakers. Nichols' own study, "Black Women in the Rural South," confirms this claim and also provides some valuable information regarding the speech of Black women. She concludes that "we must expect certain linguistic consequences to follow from the different life experiences of the two sexes. Men and women *will* speak differently from each other in every social group, but the ways and extent to which they differ can be expected to vary from social group to social group" (p. 111).

One result of the linguistic "double standard" referred to earlier is the existence of typical male and female speech styles. An example of speech which has traditionally been considered more "masculine" and less proper is the use of obscenities. In a study among Long Island college students, Anshen found that male students were twice as likely as female students to use obscenities, although there was little difference in the strength of the obscenities that were used by the two sexes. Interestingly, though, while men made a clear effort to "clean up" their speech in the presence of women, no similar effect was noticed for women in mixed company. Although they still used obscenities less often than did men, their usage did not seem at all inhibited by the presence of men. About the same time as these students were exercising their right of obscene speech, novelist Erica Jong, who was scheduled to lecture at the Smithsonian Institute, was requested twice to "keep the talk clean." Her reaction was to cancel her lecture and speak instead at a nearby college, where she delivered "a speech that would have made the Smithsonian dinosaurs rattle with fright" ("People," *Time*, Jan. 20, 1975, pp. 44-45, cited in Eble 1975b, p. 3). Today, it seems, some women are able to combat successfully attempts to silence their public speech.

The complex relationship between prestige and culturally defined notions such as politeness may be illustrated by a brief look at another culture. Elinor Keenan studied the linguistic behavior of women and men in a small village in Madagascar. This community places a high value on avoiding direct confrontation and not causing affront to others. As a result, anger, disagreement, criticism, and other negative reactions are not expressed directly. Disputes are settled through intermediaries, criticisms are "veiled in metaphor" and even orders and requests are given in an indirect fashion (p. 130). Note that this indirect polite behavior corresponds in many ways to what we consider "women's language" in our own culture. But in the community studied here, it is the men who excel in the skillful use of this type of speech. Women, on the other hand, are "norm-breakers." According to Keenan (p. 137), "they tend to speak in a more straightforward manner" and "express feelings of anger or criticism directly to the relevant party." And men use women whenever directness is needed—to ask for favors, to make direct accusations, to buy and sell in the market. The indirect speech of the men carries real prestige; there is no covert prestige attached to tough talk as seems to be true for English speakers. So we find that values are relative, but that in both the United States and Madagascar, it is the men's behavior which carries true status and prestige. Further discussion of women's politeness across many cultures in the context of a general theory of politeness, may be found in a 1980 essay by Penelope Brown. The specific examples in her study involve a Mayan community.

After this excursion overseas, let's return briefly to the American children in Fischer's study on the pronunciation

of -*ing*. Apparently, children learn different ways to speak
at an early age. In elementary school they are already
learning to "talk like a lady" and "act like a man." We find
similar results in another study of pre-adolescent children,
this one concerning pitch differences and voice quality.
There is, of course, a physical basis for the differences in
voice quality considered typical of adult women and men.
Men have larger and thicker vocal cords than women. This
in turn causes deeper voices, for the same reason that the
larger strings of a viola yield lower tones than the smaller
ones of a violin. The fact that they also have, on the
average, larger vocal tracts than women causes other
distinctions in voice quality. However, there are no
apparent characteristic physical differences between young
boys and girls which would cause differences in voice
quality, and they often sound alike. Nonetheless, in a study
by Jacqueline Sachs, Philip Lieberman, and Donna
Erickson, it was found that people were consistently able to
judge the sex of young speakers from their recorded voices,
even when the children were matched for size. Since there
is no physical basis for different ways of speaking, the
authors conclude (p. 80) that "the children could be
learning culturally determined patterns that are viewed as
appropriate for each sex." Among adults we also find that
the differences in voice quality between women and men
are greater than the anatomical differences alone would
dictate. Like children, the adults seem to be modifying
their articulation to sound more like society's ideal notions
of how women and men should sound. Such a possibility
supports the view that a society's sex-role standards
influence individuals to behave in certain unnatural ways.
It may be that, instead of reflecting linguistic reality,
accurately or inaccurately, our stereotypes actually play a
part in creating that reality.

Let's explore a bit further the ways in which this reality is
created. Little girls learn to "talk like a lady," to use good
grammar, to be polite, to avoid slang and swear words, and
to listen to boys. Boys, on the other hand, are permitted,
even encouraged, to talk rough, cultivate a deep

"masculine" voice and, if they violate the norms of correct usage or of polite speech, well "boys will be boys," although, peculiarly, it is much less common that "girls will be girls." The notion of ideal behavior for "ladies" and, to a much lesser extent, for "gentlemen," is reinforced by etiquette or courtesy books and manuals of good manners. From the fourteenth century on, women have been given similar advice to that contained in the 1970 edition of *The New Seventeen Book of Etiquette and Young Living* mentioned earlier. Not only have their parents and teachers told them how to speak, but numerous authors as well. They have been told to remain silent or speak little and, when they do speak, to be polite, gentle, and sweet, and not to gossip, curse or jest. Women are admonished not to express anger or argue, although, in the early books, they were warned to expect and accept such behavior from their husbands. In view of the fact that women were considered to be the property of their husbands, such warnings constituted appropriate survival tactics.

Here are a few examples of such advice, taken from a study of the manuals by Diane Bornstein: the Knight of La Tour Landry, who wrote his book for his daughters in 1371-72, identifies talking too much as the "second folly of Eve" (p. 132). In Luis Vives' manual of women's education, written in Latin in 1523 and translated into English in 1540, he advised women "in company to holde her tonge demurely. And let fewe se her and none at all here her" (p. 137).

Although most of these works were by men, women were so well socialized that they participated in the maintenance of the social order reflected in the manuals. One interesting woman writer of the fourteenth-fifteenth century, Christine de Pisan, herself wrote a traditional courtesy book. But she also wrote a book defending women against the antifeminists. In the introduction to this book, *City of Ladies*, she ironically states that she must be ignorant and simple indeed, for she does not find in herself or other women the faults which are claimed to be universal among women. At one point in her book, Christine asks the figure of *Reason* "why women are not allowed to act as judges. *Reason* answers that they have the intelligence and understanding, but do not have sufficient strength and verbal power" (Bornstein, p. 137).

What happens to little girls who learn their lessons well, when they grow up? Often, they receive the typical societal rewards for their femininity—admiration and respect for their good behavior, coupled with a lack of power because they are not "assertive" enough. (They also, not quite incidentally, get lower pay than men. In 1981 women earned, on the average, fifty-nine cents for every dollar earned by men.) Their speech is regarded as proper, but ineffectual and trivial. They find that the "lady-like" traits they have learned may be valued in the context of personal and family relations, but not in public and professional settings. One striking example of this is the fact that, until very recently, there were practically no female reporters on TV or radio in this country. According to Mary Ritchie Key (p. 72), a 1959 handbook for announcers explains why women announcers were not retained in radio after the Second World War: "often the higher-pitched female voices could not hold listeners' attention for any length of time, while the lower-pitched voices were frequently vehicles for an overly polished, ultra sophisticated delivery that sounded phony." "Women's delivery. . . is lacking in the authority needed for a convincing newscast."

One might now exclaim, "Wait a minute, it seems as if the women can't win." If they learn the lesson well, they are judged as stereotypically trivial and ineffectual women; if they try to change, they are "phony." This dilemma has led Robin Lakoff and others to talk about a linguistic "double-bind." We speak of a double-bind when individuals are faced with contradictory demands or expectations such that, no matter what they do, it will be wrong. Linguistically, as in other ways, a woman is "damned if she does and damned if she doesn't." Our stereotypes, our ideas about typical behavior, and our attitudes towards this behavior all conspire against women. Although this manifestation of the problem is linguistic, it is clear from the plight of women announcers described above that the solution can only come from a change in social attitudes and/or hiring patterns, not from any modification of women's linguistic practices.

Recently, women announcers have been unbound; broadcasters have bowed to societal pressures and the woman newscaster is no longer an anomaly. Similarly, Black newscasters, who were practically nonexistent in the early days of television, have joined the ranks of television newscasters in increasing numbers, especially in urban areas. We haven't seen an explicit statement regarding the unsuitability of their speech patterns for a "convincing newscast," but we do not doubt that such reasoning existed in people's minds, if not on paper. It would be interesting to investigate whether people's stereotyped notions regarding the effectiveness of the speech of women and Blacks have changed as a result of their increasing representation in the media. In the light of our earlier discussion regarding the contradictions between beliefs and reality, we suspect that old stereotypes still remain relatively unchanged, although people may now be more conscious of them as stereotypes.

Stereotyped beliefs and attitudes are not limited to the subject of women. As the above example illustrates, beliefs about ethnic and racial minorities have provoked both discussion and action in this country. For example, the slogan "Black is beautiful," was employed by the Black movement to combat negative stereotypes. Many, though not all, of the symptoms of racism in our society have parallels in symptoms of sexism. So we find that beliefs about the linguistic behavior of Afro-Americans were an important component of the widespread racist stereotypes. They included the myth of verbal deprivation and inarticulateness of Blacks, supposedly exemplified by their use of distinct dialects of English. Consider, for instance, the following description, published in 1940, of the speech of some Blacks who live in the coastal area of South Carolina and Georgia: "Its grammar, which is but an abbreviated and mutilated English grammar, knows no rule except to follow the line of least resistance, take its own tack, violate all rules of logic, and say just that which is natural and to the point." Mason Crum, the author of the passage quoted above (p. 121), describes the speech of this group as natural and to the point at the same time as he says that it violates all the rules of logic. Talk about your double binds, what do you suppose he would say about this variety of speech if it weren't natural and to the point?

People considered inferior, whether they are Black, working class, or female, are considered to have inferior speech. Whatever their speech is like, observers will interpret it as a sign of inferiority. We have just seen Crum do it. Some twenty-five years later, Carl Bereiter and Siegfried Engelmann, writing about disadvantaged, read "Black" children, blame the bulk of their problems on their speech. Seizing upon the fact that many Blacks do not pronounce the final sound of many English words, which makes it sound to speakers of other dialects as if the children run their words together into a single "giant word," they assert that Black children do not really have sentences at all and therefore cannot use the English language as a medium for thinking. If true, this would of course limit their ability to think logically. It would be no wonder that they didn't do well in school, forced to attempt to learn without the aid of language. The good doctors seem to be completely in ignorance of the fact that one of the principal differences between French and Latin is that French speakers omit the final sounds of Latin words. Despite laboring under the same handicap as do speakers of Black English, the French are often accused of being a logical people and their language is considered particularly suitable for logical thinking. Perhaps, if Black children went into wine growing, their language would be more respected.

The myths about the linguistic behavior of Afro-Americans have been completely discredited by many studies of language in Black communities. Thanks to work by Black writers and by both Black and white educators and sociolinguists, it is clear that the stereotypes of Black English were based on ethnocentric and racist misunderstandings. Contrary to earlier beliefs, Afro-American culture is highly verbal, and linguistic skills are extremely important to social status and even to survival. Also contrary to the stereotypes, Black English is not substandard English; it is a separate linguistic system, although it shares much of its vocabulary, phonology, and syntax with standard English.

The discrediting of the stereotypes has not, however, led to their abandonment. As we noted in the discussion of women's language, our beliefs tend to persist even when we "know" they are untrue. The conflict between traditional beliefs and newly discovered facts has contributed to an impassioned and often divisive debate in the Black community and the educational establishment over appropriate goals and methods. Should we recognize and/or teach Black English or incorporate Black English into our teacher training methods? Would use of Black English make it easier for Black children to master the three R's? Or would it perpetuate racism by denying Blacks full access to the standard English-speaking realms of power?

If we review the pace-setting studies by William Labov and other sociolinguists and their discussions about Black English, we discover that women are frequently either marginal or altogether absent. (There are some exceptions, such as the work of Walt Wolfram and the study by Anshen cited earlier.) Except for some findings that the speech of Black women, like that of women in other American ethnic groups, is closer to standard English than that of the men in the same groups, the studies deal almost exclusively with men. Labov et al. go so far as to state (p. 41) that "males are the chief exemplars of the vernacular culture." They explain that Black English Vernacular is spoken most consistently by adolescent boys, who were the principal subjects in their studies. Linguistically, Black women did not seem to have an existence of their own. Roger Abrahams, in his book on the language of Blacks, exclaims that "we have so very little data concerning the communication and performance habits of women" (p. 79).

A possible reason for the paucity of data on the speech of Black women might be the fact that most of the early investigators of Black English—Labov, Wolfram, Fasold, Anshen, Abrahams, and others—shared the trait of being white men. Crossing the race barrier may have exhausted them to the point that they were not up to crossing the sex barrier as well. The ideal linguistic behavior for Black women, as described by Abrahams, resembles the general cultural norm of "talking like a lady" which we have been discussing. "In general, women are expected to be more restrained than men in their talk, less loud, less public, and much less abandoned. They speak in a register closer to standard conversational English than men. Girls are lectured by both Daddy and Momma on never talking loudly or cursing, not even when involved in street encounters" (p. 69).

Although correctness and politeness form part of the linguistic norm for both Black women and middle class white women, the specific forms these take in linguistic interaction and the importance of language behavior in establishing and maintaining one's social identity are not the same for the two groups. Abrahams discusses the importance for Black women of "negotiating respect" and their use of "sweet-talk" and "smart-talk" in doing this. However, as he himself points out, the data for his discussion come almost entirely from literary and other written accounts, as opposed to the discussion of the linguistic behavior of Black men, which is based on empirical observation and recording of actual interactions. Recently, studies by Patricia Nichols, Marjorie Goodwin, and others have provided us with some empirical data on the language of Black women and girls. Hopefully, we will soon be able to see where the unique experiences of Black women set them apart linguistically and where they share in the general linguistic fate of American women.

For Hispanic and Native American women and for women belonging to other ethnic minorities in this country, we have even less information than for Black women. Some work has been done on the linguistic experience and behavior of Hispanic women, but with the exception of a few studies cited by Bodine (1975b), we know little about that of Native American women.

We have seen that Americans have many stereotyped notions about the way women speak, that many of these beliefs do not correspond to reality, and that people tend to hold on to these beliefs even though, under certain circumstances, they reveal by their behavior that they know they are untrue. Furthermore, many of the stereotypes involve negative judgments and are placed in a framework where men's speech is viewed as "normal" and women's speech as inferior or deviating in some way from the norm. The great Danish linguist Otto Jespersen found it necessary to include a chapter on "Women" in his book *Language*, but felt no need for a chapter called "Men." Men were obviously accounted for in his general discussion of language. A glance at the bibliography of our book reveals such titles as *Words and Women, Women's Language and Style,* and *Women and Language in Literature and Society.* So far as we know, nobody has ever found it necessary to write a book entitled *Men's Language and Style*; a book with that content would most likely be called simply *Language and Style.*

A similar insistence on the "abnormality" of women's behavior can be detected in political columnists' discussions of the "gender gap" after the last couple of elections, i.e., the phenomenon of men and women voting differently. Nearly all of the discussions centered on the question of why women were voting differently from men; nobody seemed to wonder why men were voting differently from women. Even where women conform to the overt standards of society more closely than do men, as in the realm of "correctness," we find there exists a covert prestige in using the more "masculine" and less "correct" forms. We can sum this up by stating that the attitudes toward women's language work to keep them in their traditional place in society.

If it were shown that men speak more surely than women, hesitating less, this would certainly be greeted as another sign of masculine superiority. The halting speech of women would be seen as evidence of their tentative, feminine nature. Yet, when Jespersen found just the opposite phenomenon, that men hesitate more than women when speaking, he naturally attributed this fact to a greater desire for accuracy and clarity among male speakers, which leads them to search for just the right word. Interestingly, when Basil Bernstein, forty years later and apparently completely ignorant of Jespersen, found that lower class young men hesitated less than upper class ones during a discussion of capital punishment, he too decided that hesitant speech was a sign of superiority. Just as predictably, Bernstein had no qualms whatever about taking his results for males and generalizing them to both sexes.

We have discussed some of the parallels between stereotypes regarding women's speech and beliefs about other groups considered "inferior" in some respect. Similarly, some observers believe that the type of speech commonly attributed to women is really characteristic of powerless groups in general, regardless of their sex. In a study of language behavior in the courtroom, William M. O'Barr and Bowman K. Atkins examined the language of witnesses of both sexes for such features as hesitation forms, use of intensifiers, and polite forms. They found that the use of the stereotypically women's language features is correlated more with social powerlessness than with sex. For both women and men, individuals with lower prestige jobs and less courtroom experience tended to use more of such features. Furthermore, experiments using transcripts of testimony with high and low frequency of these powerless features showed that witnesses using them were judged negatively—less trustworthy, less intelligent, less competent, etc. Although not directly linked to sex, powerless language was more frequent among women. The authors conclude that "women's language" and "powerless language" overlap and that (p. 109) "to speak like the powerless is not only typical of women because of the all-too-frequent powerless social position of many American women, but also part of the cultural meaning of speaking 'like a woman.'"

Communication is obviously not merely a matter of speech; it also includes facial expressions, gestures, and nonverbal behavior, usually referred to as "body language." We may use these nonverbal channels to emphasize or even contradict the meaning of the words we utter. Here too, we find stereotypes regarding the behavior of women and men, and differences between the sexes which reflect the power structures of society. As it is not possible to deal adequately with such a complex topic within the confines of this book, we have limited our discussion to verbal communication, and refer interested readers to an excellent book on the topic, Nancy Henley's *Body Politics.*

Has the women's movement had any influence on our views of women's speech? There has been an important resurgence of the women's movement in the past couple of decades. Feminist scholars have made significant theoretical contributions to many fields, including the social sciences and the humanities, and, as a result, we have come to understand better the situation of women in our society. At the same time, feminists have also advocated and participated in practical actions to improve that situation. The feminists' reaction to the question of women's language has been varied and sometimes contradictory. Firstly, we find that, as they became increasingly aware of the negative views of women's speech, women in professions dealing with language and communication began to question the prevailing myths. Past research had largely ignored women, or was based on untested assumptions about them; it often reported on male speech as if it were the speech of both sexes. It certainly seemed legitimate to try to fill in the gaps in our knowledge and set the record straight. And so a new area of language research was launched.

Many of the studies discussed in earlier sections of this chapter were carried out by women engaged in an attempt to find the truth about the differing relations of women and men to language. We have mentioned only a small proportion of such studies; since the early seventies, there has been a veritable explosion of research in this field. Francine Frank's study, "Women's Language in America," is one of several critical surveys of this research. The 1975 bibliography edited by Barrie Thorne and Nancy Henley, the most authoritative one on the subject to date, contains only twenty items from the first fifty years of this century, twelve from the decade of the fifties, thirty-four from the sixties, and eighty-one dated after 1970. A new edition of the bibliography, which appeared in 1983 in a volume entitled *Language, Gender and Society*, edited by Thorne, Kramarae and Henley, contains many more entries covering the last several years.

On the practical side, many feminists took note that women's language was believed to reflect their "natural" hesitancy and non-assertiveness. Some of them decided to adopt a masculine linguistic style. Research seemed to show that women's language, after all, is learned behavior, the result of socialization into a subordinate role. As long as men held power, their speech would represent the language of power, and it might be best for liberated women to learn this language of the powerful. It is worth noting that exactly the same arguments were being made to and by Blacks regarding the desirability of abandoning distinctively Black forms of English in favor of Standard, i.e., white, English. If men curse, but ladies don't, then the women would curse. Is men's speech generally more straightforward, direct, and result oriented than women's? The new woman would meet them on their own ground. It is difficult to say whether the women who reacted in this way were liberated or co-opted into accepting the stereotype of the superiority of men's language.

On the whole, the women who adopted this strategy, like the Blacks who adopted a similar strategy, were not rewarded with equal treatment. If a man's speech was judged to be assertive and self-confident, a woman adopting the same style would be more likely to be called aggressive and domineering. Lakoff points out that when women encroach on male territory, their diction is viewed more critically than that of men; she gives the example of the comments on the pronunciation of 'r' by Barbara Walters, the most successful of the new breed of women television reporters. Recall also the remarks about the "overly polished" and "phony" delivery of the women newscasters with low pitched voices. There are exceptions, of course, and things may improve as people change some of their traditional attitudes toward what is considered appropriate behavior for women and men. This has already begun in the field of television news, but, in general, we find that the women who have accepted the superiority of masculine style and have adopted it in their own speech, often end up without the reward they had hoped for.

Another group of women claim that adopting masculine style is not the way to true liberation and equality. They prefer to analyze the origins and functions of women's linguistic style, drawing on research like that discussed earlier in this chapter. Some of the "feminine" speech traits are best discarded as reflecting the subordinate status of women and thus being inappropriate for contemporary women. But others might well be revalued and emphasized as positive traits, worthy of emulation by men as well as women. Noting that research has concentrated largely on women's role within the linguistic domains defined by men, some people have begun to examine same-sex speech behavior among women. They have "rediscovered" traditional women's "genres" and analyzed their forms and functions, giving us studies of gossip, chitchat, and topics such as women's narratives in consciousness raising groups. Such studies, while still not numerous, are pointing the way to a revaluation of women's linguistic behavior which challenges the traditional devaluation of women's talk. In a similar vein and in the spirit of Virginia Woolf, women writers and literary critics are reexamining the traditions and views of women's writing. Those who advocate this "revisionist" policy view it as a better way for women to assume power on their own. Of course, it is true that, as long as men retain the real power, the women's style may still not be valued and accepted as valid. However, they certainly will be no worse off than the women who attempt to copy men, and they might well be better off for having created their own style and preserved their integrity. In either case, it is likely that the feminist of the future will no longer talk like the stereotypical "lady"— polite, hesitant, and ineffectual—if she has ever done so. In the final chapter of this book, we describe some of the changes that women, no longer content with merely protesting about women's linguistic victimization, have begun to advocate in order to claim for themselves an equal share in the language.

3

Hey Lady,
Whose Honey
Are You Anyway?

When we speak to one another, we reveal the nature of our relationship with and our attitudes towards the other person in many ways. One of these is in the forms of address we choose. This phenomenon is neatly summarized by Tom Sawyer when he explains to Becky Thatcher that Thomas is "...the name they lick me by. I'm Tom when I'm good."

We might well have begun this chapter with a riddle: when is an adult not an adult? Like most riddles, this is a trick question with a number of answers, one being—when the adult is a member of an oppressed racial minority; another being—when the adult is a female. Until recently, Black men in the American South were both addressed and referred to as *boy* or by their first name, especially by whites. The two forms are not unrelated. Children in our culture are universally addressed and referred to by first name; it is only as they attain maturity that they gradually come to be addressed by title and last name. By addressing Black men as *boy* and denying them last names and titles, the dominant group helped to keep the subjugated one in a powerless state of eternal childhood. Not coincidentally, white South Africans also refer to Black South Africans as *boys* and *girls*. An illustration of the devastating effect of being addressed as *boy* is provided by Peter Farb (pp. 2-3) at the beginning of his book *Word Play*, in an incident originally reported by Dr. Poussaint himself in *The New York Times Magazine* in 1967 and commented on also by Susan Ervin-Tripp:

> *The scene is a southern city in the United States; the speakers are a police officer and Dr. Alvin Poussaint, a black psychiatrist from Harvard. Exactly fifteen words are spoken in an interaction that has long been typical of black-white relations in the South:*
> *"What's your name, boy?" the policeman asked.*
> *"Dr. Poussaint, I'm a physician."*
> *"What's your first name, boy?"*
> *...As my heart palpitated, I muttered in profound humiliation: "Alvin."*

In explaining the mechanism of this insult, Farb comments: "As a speaker who belongs to the American community, the policeman was expected to use one of the three acceptable selectors: age, rank, or professional identity. Instead he selected race by addressing Doctor Poussaint as *boy*—which, of course, is a southern white man's common form of address to blacks."

Most of us can easily understand the affront involved in calling a grown man a boy, but it is considered normal and sometimes even a compliment to refer to women of any age as girls. While Frank Butler may sing yearningly of "The Girl that I Marry," it would be distinctly odd for Annie Oakley to sing of "The Boy that I Marry." Similarly, we find nothing unusual in the coach of a girls' high school athletic team addressing her team as girls, but we would be surprised to hear the coach of a boys' athletic team in the same high school addressing the team as boys. Although women in professional tennis have been among the most outspoken feminists in professional sports, it is still not unusual to hear one member of the tour refer to the "other girls" on the tour. In contrast, it is difficult to imagine John McEnroe, for example, ever referring to the "other boys"

who play professional tennis. *Girl* is so pervasive a term
that it has a variety of male counterparts in the speech of
many Americans. For a girl before puberty, the masculine
counterpart is *boy*; through high school and college age, a
male girl is usually a *guy*; and in adulthood, the male form
of *girl* is *man*. As women have been taught to value
youthfulness, many take the term *girl* as a compliment. But
the price of being eternally youthful is to never grow up,
and these women may be acquiescing in their own
powerlessness. Recently, a judge in New York State twice
addressed a lawyer appearing before him as *little girl*. The
good news is that he was reprimanded by the Commission
on Judicial Behavior. The bad news is that three of the nine
members on the commission did not want to issue a public
reprimand, while a fourth felt that the judge had done
nothing to warrant a reprimand. In the 1970's, a case
worked its way up to the United States Supreme Court
before there was a final ruling forbidding a lawyer from
addressing Black witnesses by their first names. Although
addressing women and Black men as children may be
interpreted differently by the addressees, there is a striking
similarity in the effects. Both usages confirm the
subordinate status of the group which receives this address.

It is worth noting here that the distinction between *lady*
and *woman* is quite unlike the distinction between
gentleman and *man*. *Gentleman* is simply a polite term for
a man or a term for a man of high social status or
admirable traits. Its use parallels certain uses of *lady*, as is
shown, for instance, by the polite formula *ladies and
gentlemen*, or the situation in an expensive restaurant
where a waiter might inquire "What will the lady have for
dinner?" *Lady* can also have a meaning like the second
sense of *gentleman*—somebody to be admired—in usages
such as *She is a real lady*. However, the uses of the term
lady are far more diverse and complicated than those of the
term *gentleman*. We have never dealt with a *salesgentle-
man*, neither can we inquire as to the location of the
gentlemen's room. No matter how high born a man may
be, he can never be a *gentleman poet*. In the singular,

gentleman can not be used as a term of address; one simply can't say "Hey gentleman, whose honey are you anyway?" Robin Lakoff (p. 26) suggests that the term *lady* negates the sexual aspects of a woman. This interpretation is supported by the lyrics of a country-western song which state: "I like it when you're not a lady, you drive me crazy, when we make love." However, one of the authors was listening to this song on his car radio, when a truck passed which had the message "Ladies, do you want some far out sex?" scrawled in the dirt on the back. Clearly, like the term *girl*, the term *lady* has a confusing variety of uses.

In the preceding paragraphs we have talked about addressing people and referring to them, without making a clearcut distinction between the two. There is, of course, a real difference. While we may use some terms indifferently for both purposes, such as addresssing and referring to a friend by her first name, such dual use is not always the case. Ignoring the pronoun *you*, which is always a form of address, we find that a man may refer to his female secretary as *my girl*, but he is less likely to address her as *girl*. On the other hand, he might address a group of female employees as *girls*. All of these uses of the term treat women as children, but they convey subtly different messages about the status and power relationships of the people involved. Likewise, there is a difference between referring to someone as the *lady across the street* and calling to her *Hey, lady*. Think, too, of the effect of referring to a well-known person by first name or even by a nickname. It creates an impression of intimacy that may be far from the reality. Some speakers may engage in such usage as a form of pretension, but public figures in the worlds of sports, entertainment, and politics may encourage it in their search for popularity.

We will concentrate, in the rest of this chapter, on the different ways we address women and men, reserving for the next chapter a discussion of the labels we use to refer to women. However, there will be some inevitable overlap, as in our treatment of titles and names in the present chapter.

Many languages make use of extensive and elaborate sets of address forms. These often reflect highly stratified social structures which call for constant reminders of respect, power, and social status. Japanese, for example, has a complex series of honorifics and special forms of address. In order to choose among them, a speaker must keep in mind at least the following: her own age, sex, and social status and those of the person she is speaking with, their degree of kinship, and the subject they are discussing. In Western European languages we frequently find more than one pronoun of address: speakers of French must choose between *tu* and *vous*; Germans may be addressed as *du* or *Sie*; Spaniards as *tú* or *usted*, or in some areas, *vos*; while Italians select among *tu, lei,* and *voi.* These pronouns are not, however, interchangeable forms. Depending on who is addressing whom and in what circumstances, the choice carries important social significance, not unlike that of the Japanese honorifics. As you know if you have studied one of the above languages, the proper choice among these pronouns is difficult to master, even if the linguistic forms themselves are quite simple. Indeed, Americans going abroad for the first time are often advised to use only the most formal members of these sets, on the assumption that they are likely to make mistakes and it is better to be silly than insulting. Traditionally, the different pronouns are described as formal or polite, as contrasted with informal or intimate, but each language, and sometimes different regions speaking the same language, has different rules of usage.

Pronouns of address appear to be quite sensitive to social factors, and we find that their meanings have changed over time. These changes are discussed in a fascinating article published in 1960 by Roger Brown and Albert Gilman, "The Pronouns of Power and Solidarity." Brown and Gilman suggest that, with the loosening of hierarchical social structures and the growth of democracy, the principal relationship communicated by pronoun use has changed from power to solidarity. Thus, the *tu* form has gone from its former use to address one's social inferiors to an expression of solidarity with peers, while the "polite" form has gone from its former use to address one's social superiors to an expression of social distance and politeness. As a result, usage of these forms has tended to shift from non-reciprocal exchanges marking social differences to reciprocal uses marking the degree of social solidarity. The non-reciprocal usage has not, however, completely disappeared. Age tends to command respect even if it doesn't always impart power. Adults, therefore, usually address children by the *tu* form, but can expect the more polite and respectful form in return. Within a family, a similar pattern usually prevails; sisters and brothers use *tu* to one another and the respect form to their parents. The parents, on the other hand, use *tu* to one another and to the children, while they may still address their own parents with the respect form. In some cases, families which are attempting to discard traditional hierarchical structures may adopt a reciprocal *tu* for use by everyone, thus emphasizing the solidarity and the intimacy of the family unit. Such a development is similar to an American family where the children address their parents by their first names rather than using terms like *Mother* or *Mom* and *Father* or *Dad*.

The change from non-reciprocal to reciprocal address is also complicated by the matter of sex in some of the multi-pronoun languages. Not only does the *tu* form denote solidarity, it also implies intimacy, and a girl who has always been addressed as *tu* will find, upon reaching adolescence, that some men she has known all her life will switch to the more respectful form. In addition, she will probably begin to interpret the use of *tu* by men outside her circle of acquaintances as unacceptable or even threatening social behavior. The exact meanings conveyed by the pronouns of address vary from culture to culture, but almost everywhere they continue to reflect differences in status and power between women and men.

Although the option of choosing among pronouns of address disappeared in English when *thou* became archaic, it is still possible to make socially significant distinctions of this type with various permutations of names and titles, and we find that the notions of "power" and "solidarity" and reciprocal versus non-reciprocal usage are useful in a discussion of the ways in which women are addressed in our culture. We should also keep in mind that it is quite common in English to avoid a specific form of address altogether, and that this absence may carry social meaning, usually one of ambiguity of status which the speaker has not resolved.

Many forms of address include part or all of a person's name. We have already discussed the importance of names and naming. When we address people directly, or even talk about them, we are exerting, temporarily, the power of naming. The same person may be addressed as Professor Jones, Doctor Jones, Ms. Jones, Miss or Mrs. Jones, Susan, or Susie. Each form suggests a different set of relationships, but the relationship is not determined by the one form alone; one must also know what form is returned. Thus, a different relationship is suggested by the reciprocal use of Miss Jones and Mr. Smith than by the non-reciprocal Miss Jones and Bobby.

In English, there are extensive differences in forms of address depending on the sex, age, and social position of the addressee and addressor. For a relatively formal situation where we know the person's name, a man will receive *Mr.* plus his last name. The title *Mr.* indicates politeness and the fact that the addressee is male. For women, the politeness and sexual identification are augmented by a required (at least until recently) signal of marital status: *Miss* or *Mrs.* Feminists have, of course, favored *Ms.* as a maritally neutral form of address for women parallel to *Mr.* It should be remembered that a married woman who follows the traditional practice is faced with a dizzying variety of choices. When Susan Jones marries Robert Smith, he is still limited to being Mr. Smith or Mr. Robert Smith. She, on the other hand, can choose among Mrs. Smith, Mrs. Susan Smith, Mrs. Robert Smith, and Mrs. Susan Jones Smith, and any of these with the title *Ms.* instead of *Mrs.* Any reader of newspaper advice or etiquette columns will know that many people regard the proper choice among these options as a matter of the highest import.

Children, as we have seen, are usually addressed by their first name by adults and children alike. With adults, the use is not reciprocal—adults' relative power over children and the deference they expect from children are reflected in the use of title and last name to nonfamily members, especially teachers. When a child becomes especially close to a non-family member, the solution is often not for the child to use the bare first name of the adult, but to grant the adult honorary family status so he or she may be addressed as *Uncle Bob*, or *Aunt Susan*. At some age, typically around puberty, boys begin to use last name only address among themselves and to receive this form of address from some adults, especially male teachers. This usage seems to represent in some way the boys' initiation into public life. It may also serve to identify certain settings as exclusively masculine. Just as girls are likely to continue to be called *girls* longer than boys are called *boys*, the intermediate stage of bare last names is much rarer among adolescent girls than among boys. The fact that it is used in some private girls' schools reveals that this form of address is a mark of status. In general, we find that some teachers who use last names for boys may continue to use first names for girls. At a later stage, usually in college or when they enter the world of work, young people may begin receiving the polite adult title plus last name. Here too, however, there are differences associated with sex.

Women, like children, are apt to be addressed by first name by people who expect title and last name in return. Male bosses to female secretaries and doctors to patients are notorious examples, but there are many others found in everyday interaction. Similar practices are also true of references to women; we are likely to read in a newspaper article about Billie Jean King that "Billie Jean has won three tournaments in a row," while finding out about

Jimmy Connors that "Connors has a powerful serve." The strength of the difference becomes clear if we consider a possible news story saying "Jimmy has a powerful serve." Although Miss King or Mrs. King might be substituted into the first story, only a few newspapers would be so daring as to say "King has won three tournaments in a row." As we remarked earlier, in the chapter on names, traditional newspapers like the *New York Times* insist on referring to Billie Jean King and Chris Evert Lloyd as Mrs. King and Mrs. Lloyd, and to Martina Navratilova as Miss Navratilova, even in headlines (see, for example, the July 4, 1982 story on the Wimbledon matches), while using last name only for John McEnroe and Jimmy Connors. For some reason, newspapers neutralize the *Miss/Mrs.* distinction for actresses. Elizabeth Taylor may marry, divorce, remarry, and be widowed, all the time being referred to as Miss Taylor in the public press. Some newspapers have updated their treatment of sports figures and, after a first reference which includes the full name, they use last name only for both sexes: Navratilova, King, or Connors. The *New York Times*, however, imperiously refuses women the right to name themselves and will not use the title *Ms.*, even if a woman prefers it.

There are many special address forms which do not involve a person's name. These range from "generic" forms such as *Ma'am, Sir, Miss, Mister, Ladies,* and *Gentlemen,* which signal both politeness and sex, to informal terms like *Mac, Buddy, Pal, Toots,* and *Sis,* and special "names" based on physical characteristics, such as *Shorty* and *Blondie.* In an interesting article on "Address Forms in Sexual Politics," which provides a valuable complement to earlier, essentially unisex discussions of American address, Sally McConnell-Ginet notes that not only do women receive a different set of address terms than men, but the range of expressions available for use by men seems more varied and extensive than women's repertoire. This is especially true of the informal terms of the type discussed above.

One curious aspect of generic or "no-name" address is that plural forms are generally more polite than the corresponding singular ones. Consider, for example, the difference between addressing a single individual as *boy* or *girl*, and using the corresponding plurals to a group of persons, whether children or adults. Similarly, *lady* is rarely polite and often rude as a form of address in the singular, whereas *ladies* conveys a different attitude and would be used in contexts where the singular is inappropriate.

Women can also be addressed with an offhand affection which is not allowed in addressing men. "Would you finish this up, honey?" may be used by a male boss to a female secretary without asserting any real intimacy. However, if the sex of the participants is reversed, a sense of real affection or intimacy is conveyed. Thus, a woman may be addressed as *dear* or *honey* by salespersons, service station attendants, and other strangers, both male and female. If she tries to reciprocate, it will usually be inappropriate and may be misunderstood, especially if she is speaking with a man. Nessa Wolfson and Joan Manes investigated the use of endearments to address females in service encounters in the South (Virginia) and the Northeast (Philadelphia). They found that, while the avoidance of a specific address form, as in "Can I help you?" is most common in both regions, used perhaps seventy-five percent of the time, some interesting and complex dynamics govern the use of the forms occurring in the other twenty-five percent. Not only do the sex and age of the person talking play an important role, they interact with such factors as geography and the specific situational context, to produce a bewildering variety of subtle indications of the relationship between two people. In the South, for example, older females address younger ones with an endearment more often than in the Northeast, while in the latter region, older females are more apt to be addressed as *Ma'am*. In general, sex seems a stronger influence than age in the South, with the reverse being true in the Northeast. In some cases, a switch occurred from a less intimate address term to an endearment; this seemed to be triggered by some behavior indicating the customer was not totally competent. In addition, the use of endearments seemed to permit other "intimate" speech acts such as teasing. Although salesclerks would be unlikely to tease someone they addressed as *Ma'am*, the use of *dear* appeared to give them license to do so. The authors of this study point out that the use of endearments among intimates is usually reciprocal, except with children, while their use in service encounters is non-reciprocal. They note that such contexts may be ambiguous with regard to power; it is not always the customer who wields power. The use of more intimate forms of address to women, like the use of first names, carries many potential messages, including friendliness, condescension, and expression of power. In any event, it is clear that the different treatment commonly accorded to women and men reflects their distinct social status.

In conclusion, although the English language may seem to be more egalitarian and less conscious of power differences with respect to address than languages with several pronouns of address or sets of honorifics, as speakers of English we express the dynamics of power and status in everyday interactions in many ways. These are often not favorable to women, and feminists have made a large number of people aware of the meanings implicit in some of the uses. At one extreme, unfortunately not at all uncommon, men express their economic power over women by addressing them in sexually aggressive ways. In the past, women have been faced with accepting such behavior or resigning from their jobs; recently, however, sexual harassment, including the verbal varieties, has become a legal offense. A woman who wishes to defy the traditional status relationships may choose to react to address practices by forcing reciprocal use. If she does, she runs the risk of surprising, puzzling, or even offending the person who called her *dear* or addressed her by her first name. She may, however, receive a certain amount of enjoyment out of putting him in his place and observing his reaction. According to McConnell-Ginet (p. 34), we are currently in the midst of an "address crisis." It is too early to predict the outcome, but some indication of progress may be seen in the following advice by the Ford Motor Company to its dealers (cited in the *National NOW Times*, Nov.-Dec. 1982, p. 10): "Never call a would-be buyer 'honey or dear.'"

4

Of Girls
and Chicks

English is a sexist language! Angry women have often been
driven to make such a statement. But is it accurate? Can we
really label some languages as more sexist than others? In a
recent movie, a rather obnoxious adolescent described his
favorite pastime as "cruising chicks." If the adolescent had
been female, she would not have had a parallel term to
refer to finding boys. This asymmetry in vocabulary is a
linguistic reflection of sexism in our society.

One of the more intriguing and controversial hypotheses
of modern linguistics is the idea that the grammatical
structure of a language may influence the thought
processes of speakers of that language. Regardless of the
truth of that idea, known among linguists as the Sapir-
Whorf hypothesis, it seems clear that we can gain insights
into the culture and attitudes of a group by examining the
language of that group. Eskimos live in an environment in
which the condition of snow is vital to survival, and they
therefore have a large number of distinct words for
different kinds of snow. Most Hindi speakers live in areas
of India where it does not snow and, as a result, Hindi has
only a single word equivalent to the two English words
snow and *ice*. In Modern English, the plethora of words
such as *road, avenue, freeway, highway, boulevard, street,
turnpike, expressway, parkway, lane,* and *interstate*, might
lead one to conclude that automobiles are very important
to Americans, while the relative scarcity of words for

various types of kinfolk would suggest that extended
familial relationships are not very important to Americans.
(We do not, for example, have separate words for our
mother's brother and our father's brother.) In this chapter,
we will look at the linguistic treatment of women in English
for clues to the attitudes towards women held by speakers
of English.

First let us consider what the last members of the
following groups have in common: Jack and Jill, Romeo
and Juliet, Adam and Eve, Peter, Paul and Mary, Hansel
and Gretel, Roy Rogers and Dale Evans, Tristan and
Isolde, Guys and Dolls, Abelard and Heloise, man and
wife, Dick and Jane, Burns and Allen, Anthony and
Cleopatra, Sonny and Cher, Fibber Magee and Molly,
Ferdinand and Isabella, Samson and Delilah, and Stiller
and Meara. That's right, it is a group of women who have
been put in their place. Not that women must always come
last: Snow White gets to precede all seven of the dwarfs,
Fran may follow Kukla, but she comes before Ollie, Anna
preceded the King of Siam, although it must be noted that,
as colonialism waned, she was thrust to the rear of the
billing in "The King and I." Women with guns are also able
to command top billing, as in Frankie and Johnny, and
Bonnie and Clyde. The moral is clear: a woman who wants
precedence in our society should either hang around with
dwarfs or dragons, or shoot somebody. "Women and
children first" may apply on sinking ships, but it clearly
doesn't apply in the English language.

Not only are women put off, they are also put down,
numerically and otherwise. In the real world, women
slightly outnumber men. But the world created for
American schoolchildren presents a different picture. In an
article describing the preparation of a dictionary for
schoolchildren, Alma Graham recounts the imbalance
discovered in schoolbooks in all subjects in use in the early
1970s. A computer analysis of five million words in context
revealed many subtle and not-so-subtle clues to the status
of women in American society. The numbers alone tell us a

lot: men outnumber women seven to one, boys outnumber girls two to one; girls are even in the minority in home economics books, where masculine pronouns outnumber feminine ones two to one. In general, the pronouns *he, him,* and *his* outnumber *she, her,* and *hers,* by a ratio of four to one.

When the linguistic context of the above pronouns was analyzed to see if they were generics, referring to people regardless of sex it was found that of 940 examples, almost eighty percent clearly referred to male human beings; next came references to male animals, to persons such as sailors and farmers, who were assumed to be male, and only thirty-two pronouns were true generics. In another set of words, we do find more women: mothers outnumber fathers, and wives appear three times as often as husbands. However, children are usually labelled by referring to a male parent (Jim's son rather than Betty's son), most mothers have sons rather than daughters, and so do most fathers. There are twice as many uncles as aunts and every first born child is a son. It is not altogether clear from all this how the race reproduces itself without dying out in a few generations. Notice further that, although the word *wife* is more frequent, expressions like *the farmer's wife, pioneers and their wives,* etc., indicate that the main characters are male.

Consider now another area of our language. English has a large number of nouns which appear to be neutral with regard to sex, but actually are covertly masculine. Although the dictionary may define *poet* as one who writes poetry, a woman who writes poetry appears so anomalous or threatening to some, that they use the special term *poetess* to refer to her. There is no corresponding term to call attention to the sex of a man who writes poetry, but then we find nothing remarkable in the fact that poetry is written by men. Of course, if a woman is sufficiently meritorious, we may forgive her her sex and refer to her as a poet after all, or, wishing to keep the important fact of her sex in our consciousness, we may call her a *woman poet*. However, to balance the possible reward of having her sex overlooked, there remains the possibility of more extreme punishment; we may judge her work so harshly that she will be labelled a *lady poet*. Once again, the moral is clear: people who write poetry are assumed to be men until proven otherwise, and people identified as women who write poetry are assumed to be less competent than sexually unidentified (i.e., presumably male) people who write poetry.

If the phenomenon we have been discussing were limited to poetry, we might not regard it as very significant; after all, our society tends to regard poets as somewhat odd anyway. But, in fact, it is widespread in the language. There is a general tendency to label the exception, which in most cases turns out to be women. Many words with feminine suffixes, such as *farmerette, authoress,* and *aviatrix*, have such a clear trivializing effect, that there has been a trend away from their use and a preference for *woman author* and the like. The feminines of many ethnic terms, such as *Negress* and *Jewess*, are considered particularly objectionable. Other words, such as *actress* and *waitress*, seem to have escaped the negative connotations and remain in use. However, we note that waiters often work in more expensive establishments than do waitresses, that actresses belong to "Actor's Equity," and that women participants in theatrical groups have begun to refer to themselves as "actors." On rare occasions, this presumption of maleness in terms which should be sexually neutral, works to women's advantage. If someone is called a *bastard*, either as a general term of abuse, or as a statement of the lack of legal marital ties between that person's parents, we assume that person is a male. While an illegitimate child may be of either sex, only men are bastards in common usage. Although the dictionary seems to regard this as a sex-neutral term, a recent dictionary of slang gives the term *bastarda* as a "female bastard/law, Black/" (Spears, p. 21).

Sometimes the feminine member of a pair of words has a meaning which is not only inferior to the masculine one, but also different from it. Compare, for instance, a *governor* with a *governess* or a *major* with a *majorette*. Ella Grasso was the governor of Connecticut, and a high ranking woman in the U.S. Army would certainly not be a majorette. In a large number of cases, the supposed feminine form does not even exist to refer to a woman occupying a "male" position. Women, for example, may be United States Senators, but there is no such thing as a *Senatress*. Often, where the feminine noun does exist, it will acquire sexual overtones not found in the original: compare a *mistress* with a *master*.

The last effect even spills over to adjectives applied to the two sexes. A *virtuous* man may be patriotic or charitable or exhibit any one of a number of other admirable traits; a *virtuous* woman is chaste. (The word *virtue* is, itself, derived from the Latin word for *man*.) Similarly, consider Robin Lakoff's example (p. 30) of the different implications involved in saying *He is a professional* versus *She is a professional.* Although adjectives also may come in seemingly equivalent pairs like *handsome* and *pretty*, they prove not to be equivalent in practice; it is a compliment to call a woman *handsome* and an insult to call a man *pretty*. In other cases, where pairs of adjectives exist, one term covers both sexes and the other one tends to refer only to one sex, usually females. So, members of both sexes may be *small*, but only women seem to be *petite*; both boys and girls may have a *lively* personality, but when did you last meet a *vivacious* boy?

In addition to this use of certain adjectives almost exclusively to refer to women, descriptions of women typically include more adjectives and expressions referring to physical appearance than do descriptions of men. The media clearly reflect this tendency; a report on an interview with a well-known woman rarely fails to mention that she is *attractive* or *stylish*, or to say something about her clothes or the color of her hair or eyes, even if the context is a serious one like politics or economics, where such details have no importance. Readers are also likely to be informed of the number and ages of her children. Men are not treated in a parallel fashion.

Verbs turn out to be sex-differentiated also. Prominent among such verbs are those which refer to women's linguistic behavior and reflect some of the stereotypes discussed in an earlier chapter. Women, for example, may *shriek* and *scream*, while men may *bellow*. Women and children (girls?) hold a virtual monopoly on *giggling*, and it seems that men rarely *gossip* or *scold*. There are also a large number of sex-marked verbs which refer to sexual intercourse. In their article, "Sex-marked Predicates in English," Julia P. Stanley and Susan W. Robbins note the abundance of terms which describe the male role in sexual intercourse, and the lack of parallel terms for women's role (p. 494). Women are thus assigned a passive role in sex by our language.

Another set of words which are presumably sex-neutral are the ones that end in *-man*. This suffix, which is pronounced with a different vowel from the one in the word *man*, supposedly indicates a person of either sex. It is commonly found in words designating professions—*salesman, postman, congressman*, for example—and in some other expressions such as *chairman* and *freshman*. However, the very fact that there exist female counterparts for many of these words, such as *chairwoman* and *congresswoman*, indicates that they are thought of as typically male and, as in the case of poets, when a woman is referred to, her sex must be clearly indicated. In the case of *salesman*, there are a variety of feminine forms: *saleswoman, saleslady,* and *salesgirl*. Although they appear to be synonymous, they convey significant social distinctions; someone referred to as a *saleslady* or a *salesgirl* probably works in a retail establishment such as a department store or a variety store. A woman who sells mainframe computers to large corporations would be called a *saleswoman*, or even a *salesman*. The more

important the position, the less likely it is to be held by a
-girl or a *-lady*, and the more likely it is to be the
responsibility of a *-man.*

If speakers of English often have a choice of using
separate words for men and women, of pretending that a
single word with a male marker like *chairman* refers to
both sexes, or of using a truly sex-neutral term like
chairperson or *chair*, speakers of some other languages do
not enjoy such freedom. They are constrained by the
grammar of their languages to classify the nouns they use
according to something called gender. Grammatical gender
is a feature of most European languages and of many
others as well. Depending on the language, nouns may be
classified according to whether they are animate or
inanimate, human or non-human, male or female, or, in
the case of inanimate objects, the class may depend on
shape or some other characteristic. In some languages,
meaning plays little part in determining noun class or
gender; it may be predictable from the phonetic shape of
the words, or it may be completely arbitrary. In the
European tradition, genders are labelled *masculine* and
feminine and, if there is a third noun class, *neuter.* This is in
spite of the fact that most words included in all three of
these classes represent inanimate objects like *tables* and
doors, abstract concepts like *freedom*, or body parts like
head, toe, nose, etc. Some of us English speakers may
begin to wonder about the strange world view of speakers
of languages which classify books as masculine and tables
as feminine, especially when we notice that the word for
nose is feminine in Spanish, but masculine in French and
Italian. It turns out, however, that they are not following
some animistic practice whereby inanimate objects are
thought of as having sexual attributes; in the modern
European languages at least, grammatical gender is, for
most nouns, a purely arbitrary classification, often the
result of linguistic tradition and of a number of historical
accidents. The labels come from the fact that most
nouns referring to males belong to one class and most
nouns referring to females belong to another class and,

following the human practice of classifying everything in terms of ourselves, we extend the distinguishing labels to all nouns. There are, not surprisingly, exceptions to this prevalent mode of classification, which lead to the oddity of such words as the French *sentinelle*, 'guard', being grammatically feminine, although most guards are men, while two German words for 'young woman', *Fraulein* and Mädchen, are grammatically neuter.

Are speakers of languages with grammatical gender completely straitjacketed by their grammar and forced to be sexist? We will return to this question in the final chapter. For now, we note that in these languages, the masculine forms usually serve as generics and are considered the general forms, in much the same way as the *-man* words are in English. Just as there are often alternatives to these masculine words in English, other languages also have many words that are potentially neutral and can belong to either gender, depending on the sex of the person referred to—French *poète* and Spanish *poeta* are examples, despite the dictionaries' classification of them as masculine. Yet speakers often insist on signalling the sex of women poets by adding suffixes parallel to the English *-ess, poétesse* and *poetisa* being the French and Spanish equivalents, or by tacking on the word for woman, as in *médecin femme*, one term for a 'woman doctor' in French.

Although it is true that the masculine forms serve as the unmarked or neutral terms in many languages, this does not seem to be a universal feature of human languages, as some have claimed. Iroquoian languages use feminine nouns as unmarked or generic terms; however, in the case of Iroquoian occupational terms, which are composed of a pronoun and a verb (literally translated as 'she cooks' or 'he cooks'), the sex-typing of the job determines whether the masculine or feminine pronoun is used. In Modern Standard Arabic many nouns switch to the feminine gender when they are pluralized. In many European languages, abstract nouns are predominantly in the feminine gender.

English nouns no longer exhibit grammatical gender, but the language does have a large number of words that refer to members of one sex only. In addition, when we do not know the sex of the person referred to by a noun such as *writer* or *student*, the choice of the pronoun will, as in Iroquois, often depend on culturally defined sex roles. *Teacher*, therefore, is usually *she*, while *professor, doctor,* and *priest* usually go with *he*. This brings us to the question of the "generic" use of *he* and the word *man*.

In the case of the word *man*, as in *Man is a primate*, it has been argued that this usage is independent of sex, that it refers to all members of the species, and that it is just an etymological coincidence that the form for the species is the same as that for the male members of the species. Certainly, using the same form for the entire species and for half the species creates the possibility of confusion, as those colonial women discovered who rashly thought that the word *man* in the sentence "All men are created equal" included them. More confusion may come about when we use phrases like *early man*. Although this presumably refers to the species, notice how easy it is to use expressions like *early man and his wife* and how hard it is to say things like *man is the only animal that menstruates* or even *early woman and her husband*. As with the poetical examples discussed earlier, the common theme running through these last examples is that the male is taken as the normal, that masculine forms refer both to the sex and the species, while women are the exception, usually absorbed by the masculine, but needing special terms when they become noticeable.

If the above examples have not convinced you that *man* as a generic is at best ambiguous, consider the following quote from Alma Graham (p. 62):

If a woman is swept off a ship into the water, the cry is "Man overboard!" If she is killed by a hit-and-run driver, the charge is "manslaughter." If she is injured on the job, the coverage is "workmen's compensation." But if she arrives at a threshold marked "Men Only," she knows the admonition is not intended to bar animals or plants or inanimate objects. It is meant for her.

Historically, *man* did start out as a general term for human beings, but Old English also had separate sex-specific terms: *wif* for women and *wer* or *carl* for men. The compound term *wifman* (female person) is the source for today's *woman*, but the terms for males were lost as *man* came to take on its sex-specific meaning, thus creating the confusion we have been discussing. For an authoritative opinion on the modern meaning of this word, we could turn to the *Oxford English Dictionary*, which notes that the generic use of *man* is obsolete: "in modern apprehension *man* as thus used primarily denotes the male sex, though by implication referring also to women." We note that the "modern apprehension" referred to was the late nineteenth century. If anything, the situation is even clearer today.

An even shorter word which is supposed to include women but often excludes them is the pronoun *he*. Observers have long pointed out the inconvenience of the ambiguity of this form and the advantages of having a true generic singular pronoun, which would be sex-neutral. In the absence of such a sex-neutral pronoun, speakers of English have been expected to utter sentences such as *Everybody should bring his book tomorrow*, where the *everybody* referred to includes forty women and just one man. For centuries, speakers and writers of English have been happily getting around this obstacle by using *they* in such situations, yielding sentences such as *Everybody should bring their book tomorrow*. Unfortunately, since the middle of the eighteenth century, prescriptive grammarians have been prescribing the use of *he* in these situations and attacking the use of *they*, by arguing that the use of *they* is a violation of the rule for pronoun agreement, i.e., a singular noun such as *everybody* should not take a plural pronoun such as *they*.

Although the prescriptive grammarians have not explained why it is all right for a female person such as *Mary* to be referred to by a masculine pronoun such as *he*, they have managed to make many people feel guilty about breaking the law when they use *they* in such sentences. As a result, many of us consciously avoid the use of *they* in these contexts, and some of us avoid the use of such sentences at all. Ann Bodine (p. 140) quotes a writer of a grammatical handbook advocating the latter course when faced with the need to formulate the sentence, "Everyone in the class worried about the midyear history exam, but he all passed." In 1850, an actual law was passed on the subject when the British Parliament, in an attempt to shorten the language in its legislation, declared: "in all acts words importing the masculine gender shall be deemed and taken to include females..." (Bodine, p. 136). The importance of shortening the language of legislation can clearly be seen by Parliament's use of "deemed and taken." Statements similar to Parliament's are found in leases and other legal contracts today, but, as Casey Miller and Kate Swift point out in *The Handbook of Nonsexist Writing for Writers, Editors and Speakers* (p. 37), "it was often conveniently ignored. In 1879, for example, a move to admit female physicians to the all-male Massachusetts Medical Society was effectively blocked on the grounds that the society's by-laws describing membership used the pronoun *he*." Julia Stanley (1977a) is one of a number of writers who have discredited the "myth of generics" in English. Her essay contains many examples of ambiguous and "pseudo-generic" usages.

Rather than rely on authority or opinion, some scholars have conducted experiments to determine whether or not today's speakers of English perceive the forms *man* and *he* as generic. In one study, Joseph Schneider and Sally Hacker asked some students to find appropriate illustrations for an anthropology book with chapter headings like "Man and his Environment," and "Man and his Family;" another group of students was given titles like

"Family Life" and "Urban Life." The students who were assigned titles with the word *man* chose more illustrations of men only, while the second group chose more pictures showing men, women, and children. Other studies have confirmed our tendency to interpret *he* and *man* as masculine unless the context clearly indicates they are meant generically, the contrary of what is usually claimed. One experiment, conducted by Wendy Martyna, that tested the usage and meaning of these words among young people, found that women and men may be using the terms quite differently. The men's usage appears to be based on sex-specific (male) imagery, while the women's usage is based instead on the prescription that *he* should be used when the sex of the person is not specified. Things can now run smoothly with women believing that they are included while men know otherwise.

Being treated as a trivial exception, being made to go to the rear linguistically, or even being made to disappear, are not the worst things that happen to women in the English language. Our lopsided lexicon is well supplied with unpleasant labels for women. Many, although by no means all of these, are slang words. The editor of the 1960 edition of the *Dictionary of American Slang* writes (p. 12) that "most American slang is created and used by males." This observation may be prejudiced by the fact that most collectors of American slang are males, but in any case, the words referring to women should give us an idea of the attitudes of American men towards women. The dictionaries reveal an unpleasant picture indeed.

Disregarding the obscene terms, and that is quite a task, since the list of obscene words for women is long, if monotonous, we still find term after term referring to women in a sexually derogatory way. Consider the following small sample: *chick, hussy, tart, broad, dame,* and *bimbo.* In one study, "The Semantic Derogation of Women," Muriel Schulz found over one thousand words and phrases which put women in their place in this way. She analyzes a long series of words which started out as harmless terms or had a positive meaning, and gradually acquired negative connotations. It would seem that men find it difficult to talk about women without insulting them. The opposite is not true—few of the words have masculine counterparts. After going through the lists compiled by Schulz and other writers, one may begin to wonder about the popular belief that men talk about more serious topics than do women. Unless, of course, sexual jokes and insults constitute a serious topic, men should scarcely need so many derogatory terms. An interesting, if depressing, party game is to try to think of positive labels which are used for women.

Let's examine a few examples of words for women, their meanings and their histories. The woman of the house, or *housewife*, became a *hussy* with the passage of time, and eventually the word had to be reinvented with its original meaning. So much for the dignity of housewives. *Madam* and *mistress* did not change in form, but they took on new sex related meanings, while *Sir* and *master* participate in no double entendres. Many of the most insulting words began life as terms of endearment and evolved into sexual slurs. *Tart*, originally a term of endearment like *sweetie-pie*, came to mean a sexually desirable woman and then a prostitute, while *broad* originally meant a young woman. *Girl* started out meaning a child of either sex, then took on the following meanings at various stages: a female child, a servant, a prostitute, and a mistress. The process then seemed to reverse itself and *girl* has gone back to meaning a female child most of the time, although some of the other meanings remain. *Whore*, which has the same root as Latin *carus* 'dear', referred at first to a lover of either sex, then only to females, and finally came to mean prostitute. Almost all the words for female relatives— *mother, aunt, daughter,* and the like—have at one time or another been euphemisms for prostitute. Stanley (1977b) analyzes 220 terms used to describe sexually promiscuous women. This is just a sample of a much larger group, although there are relatively few words to describe sexually promiscuous men. Even though most of the derogatory terms for women originated as positive words, some of them did not: *shrew,* for example, never had a favorable connotation.

There are many animal metaphors used to insult both men and women, *dog* being an example. However, here too, there seem to be more terms of abuse for women: *chick* is one example, another is *cow,* which has been "a rude term for a woman" since the mid 1600s according to one recent dictionary of slang. Side by side with *dog,* which can be used for both sexes, we find *bitch,* limited to women. We know of no animal terms of abuse which are limited to men. In another semantic area, there is the large group of terms used both to label and to address women as objects to be consumed: *tomato, honey, cookie, sweetiepie,* and *peach* are but a few examples. These are not necessarily derogatory and some of them, like *honey,* can be used by women to address men, but most refer largely or exclusively to women, and there is no parallel set used to refer to men. The food terms have not escaped the process of pejoration which commonly afflicts words for women, as is shown by the example of *tart,* which was included in our discussion of derogatory words.

In an earlier chapter we discussed some of the similarities between stereotypes about the way women speak and beliefs about the speech of other powerless groups. Not surprisingly, there are also many derogatory labels for such groups in the form of ethnic and racial slurs and, like women, they are the butt of many jokes. Once again we find that Black women are doubly insulted. In the words of Patricia Bell Scott, "the English language has dealt a 'low-blow' to the self-esteem of developing Black womanhood." After consulting the 1960 *American Thesaurus of Slang,* Scott states: "From a glance at the synonyms used to describe a Black person, especially a Black woman, one readily senses that there is something inherently negative about 'being Black' and specifically about being a Black woman. The words listed under the heading 'Negress,' in itself an offensive term, have largely negative and sexual connotations" (p. 220). Some of the milder terms listed include *Black doll, femmoke,* and *nigger gal.* Black women do not seem to be treated much better by Black English. Scott also examined handbooks of Black language and found "a preoccupation with physical attractiveness, sex appeal, and skin color, with the light-skinned Black women receiving connotations of positiveness." She concludes that "much of Black English has also dealt Black Womanhood a 'low-blow'" (pp. 220–21).

At the beginning of this chapter we asserted that one can determine a great deal about the attitudes of a group of speakers by examining their linguistic usage. At the end of this chapter we must conclude that the attitudes towards women reflected in the usage of English speakers are depressing indeed. They have sometimes been belittled and treated as *girls*; at other times, they have been excluded or ignored by the pretense of "generic" terms; they have frequently been defined as sex objects or insulted as prostitutes, or, on the contrary, placed on a pedestal, desexed, and treated with deference, as *ladies*. It is no wonder that many women have rebelled against being the object of such language and have become creators and advocates of new usages designed to bring equity to the English language. We will examine some of these reforms in our next chapter.

5

What Is to Be Done

At least since the time, over a century ago, when Lucy Stone decided that she would not trade her own name for her husband's upon marrying him, women and other people have attempted to change the English language so as to eliminate perceived instances of linguistic mistreatment of women. In this chapter we will consider the success of a number of these proposed changes and attempt to forecast the probable success of others. In order to do so, we would first like to consider the general issue of language reform.

Feminists are by no means the only group to work to change linguistic usage. A glance at history shows a number of cases of individuals and governments promoting language reform, with various degrees of success. Some, but not all of these, are as bizarre as the case of the French government, which has published a list of objectionable words, i.e., recent English borrowings, and established a set of fines for those French individuals and businesses rash enough to utter or print these forbidden words. Mexico, too, has launched a campaign to eliminate American expressions, such as *hello, darling*, and *honey*, from the speech of its citizens. Wisely, it has not imposed fines, but has allocated a large sum of money to an advertising campaign, using the media to combat words largely introduced through television and radio. Other

efforts to reform linguistic usage seem to us to be much
more normal. Indeed, much of the instruction in English
courses, from elementary school through the first year of
college, consists of attempts to impose new linguistic forms
on the students' native ones, usually in the name of "correct
English." A small sampling of these reforms includes: the
attempt to replace certain instances of the students' natural
use of *can* with *may;* the attempt to convince students that,
grammatically, two negatives make a positive, just as they
do in multiplication, although, strangely, three negatives
can't never be used to make no negative, despite what
mathematicians might think; and an attempt to convince
students that prepositions are not to be used to end
sentences with. Scarcely do students escape the ever-
watchful eyes of their English teachers, than they discover
John Simon, Edwin Newman, and their ilk lurking in
newspapers and television talk shows, ready to shame them
into changing even more of their natural speech. The
landscape is littered with traps: *hopefully, infer, convince
to, less, loan*, and countless others sit waiting to expose the
unwary user as illiterate and a danger to western
civilization. Cotton Mather was no more concerned with
the spiritual salvation of his flock than is Edwin Newman
concerned with the linguistic salvation of his.

Despite all this effort, school teachers and self-appointed
grammatical experts have been generally unable to
influence our spoken language in any substantial way. For
at least two hundred and fifty years, generation after
generation of school teachers has attempted to explain the
mysteries of *shall* and *will* to generation after generation of
school children, with the same blind valor and lack of
success exhibited by the Light Brigade. John Simon does
not join Jonathan Swift in condemning the use of the word
mob; this is not because the battle is won, but rather
because it is so completely lost that even these modern Don
Quixotes will not venture into the fray. Looking over the
relics of these lost causes, it might be easy to conclude that
language is impervious to outside intervention. Such a
conclusion would, however, be false. One can find a

number of instances where language has been changed by such means. Alas, such successful intervention seems rarely to be accomplished by school teachers or writers of books on how English should be used.

In Turkey in the late 1920s, the Arabic alphabet was replaced by the Roman alphabet and many Arabic and Persian words were driven from the language as a result of government decrees. Books written before these changes are today unintelligible to the vast majority of the Turkish population. In the Philippines, the national language is neither Spanish nor English, the languages of colonial rule, but Pilipino, a form of Tagalog, an indigenous language which was the native language of about twenty percent of the population. The decision to choose Tagalog was made at a national conference called to consider matters of independence. In Israel, Hebrew, a language which had been effectively dead except in the religious sphere, is now the national language, spoken by a large majority of its citizens. Again, this rebirth was brought about by conscious actions of the government and private groups. In each of the three cases mentioned above, not only did governmental policy radically affect linguistic usage, but the change was made for what can best be termed ideological reasons. In Turkey, the reform government of Kemal Ataturk wanted to turn Turkey away from what it perceived as the backward pull of Islam, towards what it perceived as the progressive aspects of western culture. In the Philippines, the government wished to emphasize the country's independence by replacing colonial languages with an indigenous one, and in Israel, the government wanted to reestablish what it regarded as a sacred language, while at the same time reaffirming Israel's national identity and unity. For similar reasons, the government of Quebec is currently in the process of promoting the expansion of the use of French in the province at the expense of English, as a way of reaffirming French culture. This is not to say that ideologically based language policy is always successful. For the last seventy-five years or so the government of Ireland has been encouraging the people of Ireland to learn and use Gaelic and to minimize the use of English. Its success can generously be described as minimal.

You do not have to be a government to affect language use. The Israeli government was greatly aided in encouraging the use of Hebrew by various Zionist groups. Americans learned to replace the term *colored* with the term *Negro* and then, a generation later, to replace the term *Negro* with the term *Black* at the insistence of the named population. Even school teachers attempting to enforce the rule against prepositions ending sentences were set upon their task largely by the efforts of a single man, Thomas Carlyle. And, as we shall see, feminist reformers of our language have scored a number of at least partial victories.

Languages change constantly; if they did not, then the residents of London would be speaking Old English today, those of Paris, Rome, and Madrid, Latin; and Athenians would be speaking Classical Greek. The vast majority of such language change is internal and undirected. Speakers of Old English, for instance, may have begun to leave out final unstressed syllables for no better reason than that it was easier to do so, but this change meant that the inflectional endings of Old English were no longer pronounced and English speakers had, therefore, to rely increasingly on word order to tell who had done what to whom. As a result of this minor change in pronunciation and its corollaries, Modern English syntax is very different from that of Old English. Such unplanned changes may affect every aspect of a language: its pronunciation, syntax, and vocabulary. The extent to which social factors influence such internal language change is still open to debate except in the area of vocabulary, where, as we have already seen, social and cultural factors have a direct effect.

Most of the changes in language usage advocated by feminists are in the area of vocabulary, with a few in the area of syntax; we know of no proposed changes in pronunciation. Some of the proposals are indicated below:

1) The replacement of the term *girl* with the term *woman* when addressing or speaking about adult females.

2) The replacement of the terms *Miss* and *Mrs.*, which are marked for marital status, by the term *Ms.*, which is as unforthcoming about the bearer's marital status as is the term *Mr.*

3) The elimination of terms such as *honey, sweetie,* etc., used in addressing women with whom the addressor does not have an intimate relationship.

4) A similar restriction on the non-reciprocal use of first names in addressing adult women, as when a doctor addresses female patients by their first names, while the doctor is called "Dr...."

5) The suppression of terms such as *chick, broad,* and similar forms in referring to women.

6) The replacement of the ending *-man* with *-person* in a large number of English words, e.g., changing *chairman* to *chairperson, congressman* to *congressperson*, etc., or the use of neutral terms such as *chair* or *representative*.

7) The elimination of needless sex distinctions exhibited by words such as *poetess* and *sculptress*.

8) The replacement of the word *man* by *human beings, people,* or some other true generic in contexts where all humans are meant, so that *man is a mammal* becomes *humans are mammals*.

9) A series of proposals with the aim of eliminating the "pseudo-generic" use of the pronoun *he*. Some advocate the introduction of a new sex-neutral third person singular pronoun such as *thon* to replace *he* in situations where either sex may be meant, as in *A doctor should be careful that thon (he) does not misdiagnose*. Others advocate the use of *he or she*, or recasting the sentence in the plural, as in *Doctors should be careful that they do not misdiagnose*. Alternatively, some women have advocated the use of generic *she*, eliminating qualms about number agreement.

10) Another proposal to eliminate the generic use of *he* by recognizing the legitimacy of using *they* or *their* with indefinite pronouns such as *someone* and *everybody*. The advocates of this proposal would favor *Everybody should button their coat* over *Everybody should button his coat*.

11) The elimination of the salutation *Dear Sir* or *Gentlemen* from business letters. A number of alternatives are proposed, including no salutation.

12) A continuation of the tradition established by Lucy Stone that married women retain their own last names, instead of taking on their husbands'. Other proposals along this line include the formation of a new combined name for both wife and husband.

In addition to the above consciously formulated proposals, feminists have coined a number of new words, such as the word *sexist* itself. The introduction of a new noun to refer to a new concept seems the easiest type of language change to bring about, often requiring little or no conscious effort. Thus, the terms *male chauvinist* and *sexism*, unheard of before 1960, are part of our language today. In the case of *male chauvinist*, a further process has taken place, whereby the term has been shortened to *chauvinist* and this newly-derived meaning of *chauvinist* is in the process of replacing the older meaning from which *male chauvinist* was itself derived. The result of this rather confusing process is that, today, someone hearing the sentence, "Smith is a chauvinist" is most likely to think that Smith is a sexist rather than the traditional meaning, Smith is a super-patriot.

Some of the new words introduced by feminists were the result of conscious efforts to articulate the previously unnamed experiences of women. Dale Spender points out that before we had the term *sexism*, "it was the behavior of women that was problematic if they were presumptuous enough to protest about the actions of some men. Without a name, the concept they were trying to present was of dubious reality... but with the name *sexism*... the reality is accepted and it is male behavior which demands justification..." (p. 184). Other examples of women's "renaming of the world," as Spender terms it, include *sexual harassment* and *phallocentric*. Words which have joined *chauvinist* in taking on new meanings include *androcentric, patriarchy,* and, more positively, *consciousness raising* and *sisterhood.* Another strategy adopted by some women has been to create new spellings like *wimmen, wymmin,* and *hystery,* as well as new coinages like *herstory,* as a way to make people think about the traditional meanings and usages of these words. Mary Daly, perhaps the most original of the feminist creators and redefiners of language, includes in her book *Gyn/Ecology,* an index of "new words," many of which are "new in a new sense, because they are heard in a new way" (p. 469). The title of her book provides a good illustration of the sort of redefinition she advocates.

Another similar change in usage is currently taking place. Many women are now using the pronoun *we* instead of *they* in contexts where they are speaking about women as a group. Such a change in pronominal use reflects a change in the speaker/writer's perspective from that of observer to that of participant. The shift in perspective is illustrated by the following examples taken from the same page of an article on women and folklore. The first identifies the writer as a feminist scholar: "But the effort to gain political power explains only one of the reasons that feminists avoid public criticism of each other. A second is that we are always seeking ways of working together..." In the second example, the author disclaims membership in the group referred to by using *they*: "Many women do not know the terms and functions of logic and argumentation; they have never learned them..." (Deemer, p. 102).

Attempts to redirect people's usage so that they choose different terms for existing concepts are more difficult to achieve, but still relatively easy in certain contexts. A number of the above proposals seek to do this. We have already mentioned the changes which resulted in the modern usage *Black*; somewhat similarly, in less than a generation, many Americans have replaced the term *girl* with *woman* when referring to adult females. The replacement of *Miss* and *Mrs.* by *Ms.* also has gained widespread, though by no means universal, currency in recent years. Its acceptance by many business mailers has been an important factor in its success, and even William Safire, a previously devoted opponent of the use of *Ms.*, declared in a recent column in the *New York Times*, "If anybody wants to sign herself as 'Ms.', I'll call her 'Ms.'" The use of *Ms.* is applauded, of course, by everybody who has ever had to address a letter to a woman of unknown marital status. The chance of social disaster with the use of *Mrs.* or *Miss* causes even the strong to quake. However, new coinages often take a while to become established and may sound odd in the meantime. Thus, some women object to the use of the term *Ms.* This has led some businesses, anxious not to offend, to give people four alternatives to choose among: *Ms., Mrs., Miss,* and *Mr.* Perhaps the most successful reform of this type has been the elimination of salutations referring specifically to men in business letters. We are much more likely today to be greeted as *Dear Customer, Dear Friend,* or with no greeting at all.

One might think that it would also be relatively easy to promote usages such as number 10 above, where what is being advocated is not really change, but the expanded use of a form which has fallen into disfavor among certain language arbiters. However, the case of sex-indefinite *they* versus generic *he* is a special and complex one. The contest has been long and controversial, and teachers and prescriptivists have invested a great deal of energy in the fight for the "correctness" of *he.* They have, as mentioned in an earlier chapter, succeeded in modifying our formal written English and in creating a collective guilty conscience among speakers of English with even a few years of schooling. But they have not managed to uproot *they* from colloquial usage and, today, some groups of feminists have unburdened themselves of their guilty conscience and are openly advocating this usage. They know that *Everybody must pay their taxes* is, unfortunately, more accurate than *Everybody must pay his taxes.* A number of books have appeared using *she* in generic situations and some writers, ourselves included, have compromised with *she or he.* *S/he* is a nice orthographic trick, but it is unusable either in the spoken language or in other grammatical cases: *her/him* and *her/his* do not collapse so neatly. Just how knotty the problem is, can be seen by trying to rewrite the sentence *Everybody is coming to the party, aren't they?* so that the verb in the main sentence agrees in number with the pronoun in the tag. *Everybody is coming to the party, isn't he?* and *Everybody are coming to the party, aren't they?* seem equally ungainly.

Because it has such a long history, the battle over *they* and *he* provides some insights into the concept of "correctness" in language and the ups and downs of conscious linguistic reform. Studies of prescriptive

grammars in English show that the earliest ones did not
single out the indefinite use of *they* as "incorrect," but that
it gradually became one of the most important "violations"
of the "rules" of grammar. As late as the last century,
English writers did not seem to be affected by a guilty
conscience in this regard, and Austen, Shaw, and
Thackeray ("A person can't help their birth") are among
those cited as setting a bad example. (Bodine discusses the
reactions of prescriptive grammarians to these writers.)

Today, for many educated people, the use of sex-
indefinite *they* is an unforgivable sin. On numerous
occasions, one of the authors of this book has been
admonished that advocating *they* would assure the failure
of any guidelines for non-sexist usage. Perhaps, then, the
teachers can claim at least a partial victory in this regard.
But the victory may be threatened. The editor of the second
edition of Fowler's *A Dictionary of Modern English Usage*
cites the *Oxford English Dictionary* somewhat disapprov-
ingly, as saying "nothing more severe of the use than that it
is 'Not favoured by grammarians' " (p. 635). He admits that
they has prevailed in colloquial usage, but states that "few
good modern writers would flout them [the grammarians]
so conspicuously as Fielding and Thackeray did... or as
Ruskin in 'I am never angry with anyone unless they
deserve it.' " Nevertheless, Miller and Swift (pp. 135–36) cite
Lawrence Durrell and Doris Lessing as among the modern
writers who have flouted the law. The most recent
Webster's New World Dictionary, Second College Edition
(Simon and Schuster, 1982) includes in its primary
definition of *they*: "also used with a singular antecedent (as
everybody, somebody, everyone)" and gives as an example
"Everybody helped and it was good that they did" (p.
1477). And finally, *Webster's Ninth New Collegiate
Dictionary* (Merriam-Webster, 1983) states that *they* is
"often used with an indefinite third person singular
antecedent" (p. 1225). The examples provided include
"nobody has to go to school if they don't want to" from
none other than the *New York Times*.

In contrast with the tortuous history of indefinite *they,* the proposals to adopt a sex-neutral pronoun have had no noticeable effect at all on people's speech habits. For over a century, feminists and others have lamented the lack of a sexually neutral third person singular pronoun in English, one which would allow us to utter sentences such as *A good doctor will always consider her patient's needs* without specifying the sex of the good doctor. A number of impassioned tracts have appeared advocating that English adopt one or another new pronominal form. One of the first to advocate such a change was Charles Converse, a nineteenth century lawyer. Although we know nothing about Converse's views regarding sexism in the language, we do know that he was disturbed by the imprecision in legal documents generated by the ambiguous use of *he* to mean *male* or *human*; he proposed *thon* for those cases where sex is irrelevant. As you may have noticed, there has been no progress made in carrying out this reform, although *thon* did appear in several dictionaries. Further, there seems little possibility that such a form will be adopted in the future despite the many brave attempts at neologism. Dennis Baron's study of suggestions for neutral pronouns lists some thirty-five proposals, including *thon, shim,* and *hir.* Apparently, while inventing new pronominal forms is an easy task, convincing people to use them is much more difficult than replacing one existing pronoun with another. The Quakers have discovered that it is also extremely difficult to revive obsolete pronouns such as *thee* and *thou.* Even such usages as *he or she, he/she,* and *s/he,* combining existing forms, while not sweeping the country, do have more currency than forms such as *thon.*

The attempted change of -*man* words seems to have had a variety of results. In some cases, such as *chair* or *chairperson,* the change has been relatively accepted by a portion of the population, although the latter term is often reserved for women who chair meetings or departments. In other cases, such as *freshperson,* the alternate forms seem not to exist at all in spontaneous usage. It may be that there is a wide range of differences among words of the form *X-man*, with some, such as *chairman*, being interpreted as 'a man who is X,' and others, such as *freshman*, being interpreted as 'a person who is X.' One major step in the replacement of *-man* words by sex-neutral forms was the adoption of new names for occupations by the United States Department of Labor. These changes were incorporated in the 1977 edition of the *Dictionary of Occupational Titles*. Some of the changes are: from *airline steward* and *stewardess* to *flight attendant*, from *fisherman* to *fisher*, *hat-check-girl* to *hat-check attendant*, *maid* to *house worker*, and *watchman* to *guard*. *Roget's Thesaurus* has also adopted sex-neutral terminology in its latest edition. Of course, the official sanctioning of the common gender words does not guarantee their acceptance in everyday usage, but it isn't likely to hurt. Lest anyone think such matters are trivial, it is worth mentioning that a number of studies have shown that young people are influenced in their job preferences and their willingness to apply for advertised jobs by gender bias in the wording of the advertisements. (See, for example, Sandra L. Bem and Daryl J. Bem, 1973.)

In an earlier chapter, we discussed the grammatical category of gender, which forces speakers of some languages to identify nouns referring to people as masculine or feminine. It is more difficult in such languages to find alternative sex-neutral forms such as the English *firefighter*. Although it would seem futile to propose that speakers of languages like Spanish and French abandon the use of gender, changes are occurring in these languages. We find, for example, that feminists are advocating the use of a single term as an occupational title, with either masculine or feminine agreement forms. So a poet would be referred to in Spanish as either *un poeta* or *una poeta*, depending on sex, rather than *un poeta* and *una poetisa*. These changes are similar to the ones proposing the abandonment of English words with feminine suffixes.

Regarding the proposal that women retain their own name at marriage, one might think that this would be the easiest change of all. After all, what is being advocated is that something *not* change. Further, English Common Law has always recognized the right of an individual to use any name she or he wishes, as long as there is no intent to defraud anybody. And indeed, the custom of not changing one's name is being adopted by a growing number of American women. However, as we discussed earlier in the chapter on names, this trend seems to have engendered a considerable amount of hostility. We also note a substantial number of women who follow the less controversial practice of using both their husband's last name and their own, depending on the situation. They may use their own last name in business situations and their husband's name with friends and family, especially his. Telephone books provide interesting data on recent trends in this area. Many now list both first names for a married couple, as in Jones, John and Mary. We also find that women frequently choose to have a separate listing under their own name, and in a few instances, a new sort of entry has appeared, such as Jones, John and Mary Smith.

The power of the printed word was recognized by feminists early in the campaign for non-sexist language. Accordingly, they promoted the adoption of editorial policies and guidelines for non-sexist writing by publishers and professional associations. In many cases, especially that of textbook publishers, such guidelines were designed to avoid ethnic and class bias as well as stereotypes based on sex. The guidelines include many of the proposals specified above; in addition, they caution against using language which limits women and men to traditional sex roles and sex-typed behavior, or omits women altogether. Girls, therefore, are allowed to fix things and be adventurous, while boys may feel emotion and even cry. Among the groups which follow guidelines of this type are many publishers of textbooks for elementary and secondary schools, The American Psychological Association, The National Council of Teachers of English, The International Association of Business Communicators, and a number of religious organizations. Some states have also determined to change the wording of legislation so as to make it non-sexist.

Like the proposals concerning the spoken language, proposed language changes of this kind may be met with both general conservatism deploring anything which might besmirch the "purity" of the language, and specific resistance to the idea that women are badly treated in English. It is often difficult to distinguish the two types of critics. Ridicule is a favorite weapon of such people and much fun has been made of such supposed forms as *personfacture* and *girlcott*. Other criticisms of the reforms range from accusations of censorship to statements that the matter is too trivial for feminists to be wasting their time in this way. Nevertheless, the guidelines are having an effect, and a comparison of elementary and high school textbooks published in the late sixties with more recent books will turn up far fewer examples of blatant sexism in the new books. In other areas, such as newspapers and academic or scholarly writing, the record is more uneven. As we have indicated earlier, the *New York Times* steadfastly refuses to change with the times; some other newspapers, however, have adopted sex equity in language as editorial policy. A number of religious groups have also responded positively to the campaign for non-sexist usage. One such organization, The United Presbyterian Church in the U.S.A., has resolved to revise church documents to replace "generic usages of masculine nouns, pronouns, and adjectives" by language which includes both sexes and affirms "the full personhood of all."

We argued earlier that sexist usages in language are primarily a reflection, rather than a cause, of sexist attitudes in society; they will probably die out naturally as the society becomes less sexist. This does not mean that we believe it is a waste of time to attempt to change sexist usages. On the contrary, we see at least two important benefits from such a struggle. First, the struggle itself increases awareness of the sexual inequalities in the society upon which these usages are based. We tend to accept what is as natural; it is only after somebody has asked us why women have no permanent names of their own that we may begin to question the nature of a society which denies women the right to their own names. Second, the power to determine linguistic usage has in the past been reserved largely to men; by participating in the reform of sexist usage, women have begun to appropriate some of that power to themselves. They have begun to add to our language terms which describe women's experience from women's own point of view. This has enabled them to articulate their past oppression, and having a name for it has helped empower women to combat this oppression. Language is the common heritage of humans; all humans must share in shaping and using it.

Suggested Research Projects

It is only in the last ten to twenty years that the linguistic distinctions between the sexes have been studied in anything but the most cursory fashion and not much longer that these distinctions were treated as anything more than female "deviations" from the (male) norm. Although much work has been done in the last two decades, much more remains to be done. In this chapter, we wish to suggest a few areas of study, some of which may be appropriate as class projects. We have included suggestions relevant to most of the chapters in the book.

Naming Names

One area of possible research is that of names. Many of the claims made in the first chapter about men's and women's names are based on Larm's study, which took place in Hawaii. Are her findings generalizable to other areas of the United States, are there similar phonological traits associated with feminine and masculine names in languages other than English? We could measure people's reactions to an article written by "Lisa Smith" versus the same article if the author were called "Joan Smith." An interested researcher should be able to find data on how styles in names have changed over time. Are there systematic or only random differences between men's and

95

women's names in the nineteenth century and in the twentieth century, do these differences have any significance? To what extent is the practice of women not taking their husband's last name expanding?

Oral histories and interviews may provide interesting data about names and our feelings toward them. Some topics for such interviews include asking people how they feel about their own names, whether they would ever change their first and/or last name and under what circumstances, how they would react if someone close to them did so, and asking parents how they chose names for their children. If you know people who have changed their name for political or personal reasons, women who have maintained their own name after marriage, or families with combined names, you can ask about motivations for their name changes, obstacles which they have met, and consequences of their decision.

Another area for research concerns names for inanimate objects. Examples can be collected and classified by gender of the names and type of object (cars, computers, etc.); people can be interviewed regarding reasons for naming a particular object and the choice of name.

Genealogies have become a favorite pastime for many people. If you or a relative or friend have a family history, see if our claims about the duration of names are borne out. When are the family names of the women lost as compared to those of the men?

Talking Like a Lady

There is still a great deal to be learned about the extent to which women and men use language differently. Can the speech of men and women be consistently differentiated, if differences in voice quality are neutralized? Sonder's study utilizing transcripts of discussion groups gives us some data on the subject, but certainly does not answer all of our questions. What about less formal situations, what about speakers from different socio-economic classes? Can we get some insight into this problem from other sources, letters to the editor, fictional works, or the like? If men and women are asked to respond to the same stimulus, for instance, asked to describe a picture, will their responses be distinguishable? Some previous research indicates that they do respond differently. If men and women can be identified to a certain extent by their linguistic usage, just what are the differences—do they lie in word choice, use of adjectives, total number, content, variety of words used? As well as using real people as the subjects of these studies, one can get at some of the facts in other ways. It is possible, for instance, to look at representations of women's and men's speech in plays and novels. Although there are some obvious problems of accuracy in the representations, the relative accessibility of the data may compensate.

People, of course, do not speak in a vacuum; although we may talk to ourselves on occasion, we use language mainly to interact with other people. Observations of such normal communicative events can yield many insights into sex differences in speech and what functions they serve. Who interrupts whom, who initiates topics of conversation, who does the work of carrying on the conversation? One must be careful to take into account relationships between the people involved such as power, age, social and economic status. Do your observations tend to confirm the overlap between what is usually labelled "women's language" and what some have termed "powerless language?" Are women changing their speech? Observation of speech and interactions involving successful and/or "liberated" women may reveal interesting trends; interviews could indicate whether changes noted are a matter of conscious choice.

Have our preconceived notions about women's and men's speech changed with the changes in the status and roles of women? How do we react to the language of women newscasters on television, for example? One might ask people to characterize the speech of women newscasters in general and of specific women, and compare the results with reactions to the speech of men on television news programs.

Hey Lady, Whose Honey Are You Anyway? and Girls and Chicks

(Forms of address and forms of reference)

People are much more self-conscious about referring to adult women as *girls* than they once were. However, this usage is still widespread. Is there some way to determine the extent to which customs have changed and the extent to which people still rely on the old usage? The meanings of the word *lady* range from the admiring, "She's a real lady," to the patronizing, "She was a lady novelist." Can the entire range of meanings be determined and what are the distinguishing features of each? What would happen if one looked at the definition of *lady* in a variety of dictionaries? Do counterparts in other languages, such as French, Spanish and German have the same range of meanings?

The use of endearments in service and other casual encounters and the meanings implicit in such usage varies, as we have noted, from one region to another. In some parts of England, for example, working class people use *love* and *ducks* as forms of address in service encounters. In this country, in addition to the regional differences, there are also ethnic and class differences in the use of terms like *honey*. An interesting topic for a group research project would be systematic observation of forms of address in specific interaction contexts and an attempt to analyze differences based on sex, age, class, relative power, status, and other relevant characteristics of addressor and addressee. The essential difference between reciprocal and non-reciprocal address should be kept in mind.

We commented on the practice of many publications of referring to women by their first names or by their title and last names, while referring to men by their last names. It is also common to add descriptive notes on women's personal

appearance—*matronly Margaret Thatcher*, for example—
or their family status—*Mother of three arrested in sit-in.*
Again, it would be interesting to quantify this tendency,
determine which publications are the worst offenders, and
see if there are any measurable changes going on. The same
sort of study could be done based on usage on television
and radio news.

We have entered an era of computers and robots. Does
linguistic usage in these new areas of our lives show an
awareness of societal change as far as the situation of
women is concerned, or does it reflect the same old
stereotypes? In a recent television interview concerning
robots, discussion turned to a robot developed by the
Heathkit company. Its name was Hero I and it was
consistently referred to as *he*, and described as "the
grandfather of future robots." Is this typical?

What Is to Be Done

How is the use of titles such as *Mr., Ms.*, etc., evolving? Is
usage changing in this respect in people's speech, in
writing, in the media? What is the trend in the use of sex-
neutral terms as opposed to the -*man* words, of *he* vs. *they*?
Mini-surveys on such topics should reveal a great deal
about the relationship between language and social change,
as will interviews regarding people's attitudes and reactions
to the changes in usage mentioned in this chapter and in
our sample guidelines.

Bibliography

Abrahams, Roger. *Talking Black.* Rowley, Mass.: Newbury House, 1976.

Anshen, Frank. "Speech Variation among Negroes in a Small Southern Community." Ph.D. dissertation, New York University, 1969.

Anshen, Frank. "Sex and Obscenity at Stony Brook." Unpublished manuscript, State University of New York at Stony Brook, 1974.

Baron, Dennis E. "The Epicene Pronoun: The Word that Failed." *American Speech* 56(2) (1981): 83-97.

Bem, Sandra L. and Daryl J. Bem. "Does Sex-biased Job Advertising 'Aid and Abet' Sex Discrimination?" *Journal of Applied Social Psychology* 3 (1973): 6-18.

Bereiter, Carl and Siegfried Engelmann. *Teaching Disadvantaged Children in the Preschool.* Englewood Cliffs, N.J.: Prentice-Hall, 1966.

Bernstein, Basil. "Social Class, Linguistic Codes and Grammatical Elements." *Language and Speech 5* (1962): 221-250.

Bodine, Ann. "Androcentrism in Prescriptive Grammar: Singular 'They,' Sex-Indefinite 'He' and 'He or She'." *Language in Society* 4 (1975)(a): 129-146.

Bodine, Ann. "Sex Differentiation in Language." In *Language and Sex: Difference and Dominance*, edited by Barrie Thorne and Nancy Henley, pp. 130-151. Rowley, Mass.: Newbury House, 1975(b).

Bornstein, Diane. "As Meek as a Maid: A Historical Perspective on Language for Women in Courtesy Books from the

Middle Ages to Seventeen Magazine." In *Women's Language and Style,* edited by Douglas Butturff and Edmund L. Epstein, pp. 132-138. Akron, Ohio: L & S Books, 1978.

Brown, Penelope. "How and Why Are Women More Polite: Some Evidence from a Mayan Community." In *Women and Language in Literature and Society,* edited by Sally McConnell-Ginet, Ruth Bowker and Nelly Furman, pp. 111-136. New York: Praeger, 1980.

Brown, Roger and Albert Gilman. "The Pronouns of Power and Solidarity." In *Style in Language,* edited by Thomas A. Sebeok, pp. 253-276. Cambridge, Mass.: MIT Press, 1960. (Reprinted in Joshua A. Fishman, ed. *Readings in the Sociology of Language.* The Hague: Mouton, 1968. Also in Pier P. Giglioli, ed. *Language and Social Context.* Harmondsworth, England: Penguin, 1972.)

Crum, Mason. *Gullah: Negro Life in the Carolina Sea Islands.* Durham, N.C.: Duke University Press, 1940. (Reprinted in 1968 by Negro Universities Press, New York.)

Daly, Mary. *Gyn/Ecology: The Metaethics of Radical Feminism.* Boston: Beacon Press, 1978.

Deemer, Polly Stewart. "A Response to the Symposium." *Journal of American Folklore* 88 (1975): 101-109.

Eble, Connie C. "Girl Talk: A Bicentennial Perspective." Unpublished manuscript, University of North Carolina at Chapel Hill, 1975(a).

Eble, Connie C. "If Ladies Weren't Present I'd Tell You What I Really Think." Unpublished manuscript, University of North Carolina at Chapel Hill, 1975(b).

Edelsky, Carole. "Acquisition of an Aspect of Communicative Competence: Learning What It Means to Talk Like a Lady." In *Child Discourse,* edited by Susan Ervin-Tripp and Claudia Mitchell-Kernan, pp. 225-243. New York: Academic Press, 1977.

Ervin-Tripp, Susan. "On Sociolinguistic Rules: Alternation and Co-occurrence." In *Directions in Sociolinguistics*, edited by John J. Gumperz and Dell Hymes, pp. 213-250. New York: Holt, Rhinehart & Winston, 1972.

Farb, Peter. *Word Play.* New York: Alfred A. Knopf, 1974. (Bantam, 1975.)

Fasold, Ralph W. *Tense Marking in Black English.* Arlington, Va.: Center for Applied Linguistics, 1972.

Fischer, John L. "Social Influence in the Choice of a Linguistic Variant." *Word* 14 (1959): 47-56. (Reprinted in Dell Hymes, ed. *Language in Culture and Society.* New York: Harper and Row, 1964.)

Fishman, Pamela M. "What Do Couples Talk about When They're Alone?" In *Women's Language and Style,* edited by Douglas Butturff and Edmund L. Epstein, pp. 11-22. Akron, Ohio: L & S Books, 1978.

Fowler, H.W. *A Dictionary of Modern English Usage* 2nd ed., rev. by Sir Ernest Gowers. New York: Oxford University Press, 1965.

Frank, Francine Wattman. "Women's Language in America: Myth and Reality." In *Women's Language and Style,* edited by Douglas Butturff and Edmund L. Epstein, pp. 47-61. Akron, Ohio: L & S Books, 1978.

Goodwin, Marjorie Harness. "Directive-Response Speech Sequences in Girls' and Boys' Task Activities." In *Women and Language in Literature and Society,* edited by Sally McConnell-Ginet, Ruth Borker and Nelly Furman, pp. 157-173. New York: Praeger, 1980.

Graham, Alma. "The Making of a Nonsexist Dictionary." In *Language and Sex: Difference and Dominance,* edited by Barrie Thorne and Nancy Henley, pp. 57-63. Rowley, Mass.: Newbury House, 1975.

Haas, Mary. "Men's and Women's Speech in Koasati." *Language* 20 (1944): 142-149. (Reprinted in Dell Hymes, ed. *Language in Culture and Society.* pp. 228-232. New York: Harper and Row, 1964.)

Haupt, Enid A. *The New Seventeen Book of Etiquette and Young Living.* New York: David McKay, 1970.

Henley, Nancy. *Body Politics: Power, Sex, and Nonverbal Communication.* Englewood Cliffs, N.J.: Prentice-Hall, 1977.

Holm, John. "The Creole English of Nicaragua's Miskito Coast: Its Sociolinguistic History and a Comparative Study of its Lexicon and Syntax." Ph.D. dissertation, University of London, 1978. (Ann Arbor, Michigan: University Microfilms 8208, 490.)

Jespersen, Otto. *Language: Its Nature, Development and Origin.* London: Allen and Unwin, 1922. (See chap. 13, "The Woman," pp. 237–54.)

Keenan, Elinor. "Norm-Makers, Norm-Breakers: Uses of Speech by Men and Women in a Malagasy Community." In *Explorations in the Ethnography of Speaking*, edited by Richard Bauman and Joel Sherzer, pp. 125-143. New York: Cambridge University Press, 1974.

Key, Mary Ritchie. *Male/Female Language.* Metuchen, N.J.: Scarecrow Press, 1975.

Kramarae, Cheris. *Women and Men Speaking.* Rowley, Mass.: Newbury House, 1981.

Labov, William, Paul Cohen, Clarence Robins and John Lewis. "A Study of the Non-Standard English of Negro and Puerto Rican Speakers in New York City." Report on Co-operative Research Project 3288. New York: Columbia University, 1968.

Lakoff, Robin. *Language and Woman's Place.* New York: Harper and Row, 1975. (Part 1 reprinted from *Language in Society* 2 (1973): 45–79.)

Larm, Carol. "What Shall We Name the Baby." Unpublished manuscript, 1979.

McConnell-Ginet, Sally. "Address Forms in Sexual Politics." In *Women's Language and Style*, edited by Douglas Butturff and Edmund L. Epstein, pp. 23-35. Akron, Ohio: L & S Books, 1978.

Martyna, Wendy. "The Psychology of the Generic Masculine." In *Women and Language in Literature and Society*, edited by Sally McConnell-Ginet, Ruth Borker and Nelly Furman, pp. 69-77. New York: Praeger, 1980.

Miller, Casey and Kate Swift. *Words and Women: New Language in New Times.* Garden City, N.Y.: Anchor Press/Doubleday, 1976.

Miller, Casey and Kate Swift. *The Handbook of Nonsexist Writing.* New York: Lippincott & Crowell, 1980.

Newell, Holly. "A Study of Nicknames." Unpublished manuscript, 1975.

Nichols, Patricia C. "Black Women in the Rural South: Conservative and Innovative." In *The Sociology of the Languages of American Women: Papers in Southwest English* 4, edited by Betty Lou Dubois and Isabel

Crouch, pp. 103–114. San Antonio: Trinity University 1976.

O'Barr, William M. and Bowman K. Atkins. "'Women's Language' or 'Powerless Language'?" In *Women and Language in Literature and Society,* edited by Sally McConnell-Ginet, Ruth Borker and Nelly Furman, pp. 93-110. New York: Praeger, 1980.

Oliver, Robert T. *History of Public Speaking in America.* Boston: Allyn & Bacon, 1965.

Sachs, Jacqueline, Philip Lieberman and Donna Erickson. "Anatomical and Cultural Determinants of Male and Female Speech." In *Language Attitudes: Current Trends and Prospects,* edited by Roger W. Shuy and Ralph W. Fasold, pp. 74-84. Washington, D.C.: Georgetown University Press, 1973.

Sapir, Edward. "Male and Female Forms of Speech in Yana." In *Selected Writings of Edward Sapir,* edited by David Mandelbaum, pp. 206-212. Berkeley: University of California Press, 1949.

Schneider, Joseph and Sally Hacker. "Sex Role Imagery and Use of the Generic 'Man' in Introductory Texts: A Case in the Sociology of Sociology." *The American Sociologist* 8 (1973): 12-18.

Schulz, Muriel R. "The Semantic Derogation of Women." In *Language and Sex: Difference and Dominance,* edited by Barrie Thorne and Nancy Henley, pp. 64-75. Rowley, Mass.: Newbury House, 1975.

Scott, Patricia Bell. "The English Language and Black Womanhood: A Low Blow at Self-esteem." *The Journal of Afro-American Issues* 2 (1974): 218-225. (Reprinted in Willa Johnson and Thomas Greene, eds. *Perspectives on the Afro-American Woman.* Washington, D.C.: ECCA Publications, 1975.)

Sonder, Otto. "An Experimental Study of the Identification of the Sex of Discussion Group Participants." Ph.D. dissertation, Pennsylvania State University, 1964.

Spears, Richard A. *Slang and Euphemism.* Middle Village, New York: Jonathan David, 1981.

Spender, Dale. *Man Made Language,* London: Routledge & Kegan Paul, 1980.

Stanley, Julia P. "Gender-Marking in American English: Usage and Reference." In *Sexism and Language*, edited by Alleen Pace Nilsen, Haig Bosmajian, H. Lee Gershuny and Julia P. Stanley, pp. 43-74. Urbana, Ill: National Council of Teachers of English, 1977(a).

Stanley, Julia P. "Paradigmatic Woman: The Prostitute." In *Papers in Language Variation*, edited by David L. Shores and Carole P. Hines, University, Ala: University of Alabama Press, 1977(b).

Stanley, Julia P. and Susan W. Robbins. "Sex-marked Predicates in English." *Papers in Linguistics* 11 (3-4) (1978): 487-516.

Stannard, Una. *Mrs. Man.* San Francisco: Germainbooks, 1977.

Thorne, Barrie and Nancy Henley, eds. *Language and Sex: Difference and Dominance.* Rowley, Mass.: Newbury House, 1975.

Thorne, Barrie, Cheris Kramarae and Nancy Henley, eds. *Language, Gender and Society.* Rowley, Mass.: Newbury House, 1983.

Trudgill, Peter. "Sex, Covert Prestige and Linguistic Change in the Urban British English of Norwich." *Language in Society* 1 (1972): 179-195. (Reprinted in Barrie Thorne and Nancy Henley, eds. *Language and Sex: Difference and Dominance.* Rowley, Mass.: Newbury House, 1975.)

The United Presbyterian Church in the U.S.A. *The Power of Language among the People of God and the Language about God "Opening the Door."* New York: Advisory Council on Discipleship and Worship, 1979.

Wolfram, Walt. *A Sociolinguistic Description of Detroit Negro Speech.* Washington, D.C.: Center for Applied Linguistics, 1969.

Wolfson, Nessa and Joan Manes. " 'Don't "Dear" me!' " In *Women and Language in Literature and Society*, edited by Sally McConnell-Ginet, Ruth Borker and Nelly Furman, pp. 79-92. New York: Praeger, 1980.

Zimmerman, Don H. and Candace West. "Sex Roles, Interruptions and Silences in Conversation." In *Language and Sex: Difference and Dominance,* edited by Barrie Thorne and Nancy Henley, pp. 105-129. Rowley, Mass.: Newbury House, 1975.

Guidelines
for
Non-Discriminatory
Language Usage

The following suggestions for non-sexist language use provide a summary of the major questions of usage dealt with in the text. While they are not meant to be comprehensive, we hope that these guidelines will prove to be a useful and usable quick reference for those readers interested in adopting non-sexist usage. Many of the suggestions also appear in the guidelines adopted by publishers and other groups, and in more detailed manuals such as Miller and Swift's *Handbook of Nonsexist Writing*.

We have found it useful to adopt the distinction between questions of designation and questions of evaluation which appears in the "Guidelines for Nonsexist Language" of the American Psychological Association. Questions of designation include language usage which is ambiguous as to whether one or both sexes is being referred to, as well as language which reflects stereotypes regarding sex roles. Thus, the use of "generic" *he* to refer to *the child* is an example of ambiguous designation, whereas use of *he* to refer to *the doctor* and *she* to refer to *the nurse* reflects both ambiguity and stereotyped designation. Questions of evaluation often involve common clichés and other expressions which are so familiar that we may not readily recognize the sexism implicit in the usage. Examples include the use of non-parallel expressions such as *men and girls* when referring to adults of both sexes, use of different adjectives to describe the same characteristics—*cautious men* but *timid women*, labelling of women, but not men, by adjectives or nouns—*woman driver, blond secretaries,* etc.

Questions of Designation

Ambiguity. Unintentional ambiguity can cause misunderstanding and confusion and, as we have seen, may also be discriminatory. Where references to sex and sex roles are concerned, one can avoid such consequences by following two suggestions: (1) use neutral or universal terms when referring to both sexes and where the sex of the person referred to is not relevant; (2) use sex-specific terms only when referring specifically to women or men.

(1) Use of universal terms to refer to people in general

INAPPROPRIATE	SUGGESTED ALTERNATIVES

a. Pronouns

We hope the *reader* will use *his* own judgment.	We hope *you* will use *your* own judgment. *or* We hope *readers* will use *their*l own judgment.
The *child* is influenced by *his* peers.	*Children* are influenced by *their* peers. *or* Peer influence is an important factor for a child.

b. Man, mankind, compounds with *-man*

The average *man* votes according to *his* self interest.	The average *person* votes according to self interest. *or* *People* vote according to (*their*) self interest.
An important step for *mankind.*	An important step for *humanity.*

INAPPROPRIATE	SUGGESTED ALTERNATIVES
Write to your *congressman* today.	Write to your (*congressional*) *representative* today. *or* *member of Congress*
workman	worker
policeman	police officer
mailman	mail (letter) carrier
chairman	chair, chairperson etc.

c. Salutations for letters

Dear Sir
Gentlemen
	no salutation (impersonal business letter where name of person is unknown)
	or
	Dear *(Name)*
	        Jane Rogers
	        Ms. Leone
	        Mr. Kaplan
	or
	Dear *(functional title)*
	        Credit Manager
	        Customer
	        Colleague, etc.
	(where individual is unknown, but function is pertinent)

It should be noted that the alternatives suggested above involve a number of different processes. In some cases, simple substitution of a universal term such as *humanity* for an ambiguous generic such as *mankind* is sufficient. Some sentences may be recast in the plural, while in others the inappropriate pronoun is unnecessary as it carries no meaning. In still other instances, an alternative sentence structure avoids the possible ambiguity. We have given only a few examples to illustrate the processes—the list of alternatives could have been much longer. One common usage not mentioned above is the use of *she or he, his or her*, and *him or her* when a pronoun seems unavoidable. Some people object to repeated use of these expressions as "clumsy," and it sometimes does represent a "lazy way out." Occasional use of *he or she*, however, is perfectly acceptable to most people. Forms such as *he/she* or *s/he* have been adopted by some writers, but they have no natural counterparts in the spoken language.

(2) Use of sex-specific terms

The use of appropriate universal terms assures that sex-specific terms will be understood unambiguously. Thus, if we state that college-educated men earn more than those with a high school education, it will be clear that we are not referring to women. Likewise, if we wish to compare women and men in the same profession, the use of such terms as *female* or *women doctors* alongside of *male* or *men doctors* is appropriate.

Questions of Evaluation

Avoiding the sexism in expressions referring to women which involve derogatory connotations, evaluation of women as inferior, and other stereotypes, is not as simple as avoiding sexist designations. Designation is often a matter of specific linguistic forms, while problems of evaluation require a recognition of the negative stereotype or attitude behind the usage. Context, both linguistic and societal, plays a more important role in questions of evaluation. There are, of course, many instances of sexist usage which involve both designation and evaluation.

(1) Asymmetrical constructions vs. parallel terms

INAPPROPRIATE	SUGGESTED ALTERNATIVES
man and wife	husband and wife (Both terms refer to a relationship.)
Mr. Jones and his family	The Jones family
Mr. Lucas and his wife Louise	Sam and Louise Lucas
	or
	Louise and Sam Lucas
	(Women and children are not viewed as possessions of men.)

INAPPROPRIATE	SUGGESTED ALTERNATIVES
Addressing or referring to male members of a group as *men* and female members as *girls*	Either *women and men* or *boys and girls*, according to the situation. (Many people who object to the use of the term *lady* point out that it is not parallel to *man*.

It is also appropriate to reverse the order of some traditional expressions so that women do sometimes precede men, e.g., *women and men, her or his*. |
| Referring to a woman by title (Ms. King) and to a man by last name only (McEnroe) in the same context | Ms. King and Mr. McEnroe or Billie Jean King and John McEnroe or King and McEnroe |

(2) Unnecessary reference to sex in designating people

INAPPROPRIATE	SUGGESTED ALTERNATIVES
	Universal or neutral terms:
poetess	poet
sculptress	sculptor
waitress	waiter or server
male nurse	nurse
lady mayor	mayor

The suggested alternative usage for the above category of words is identical to the usage recommended for the *-man* terms in the section on designation. The problem here, however, is not one of ambiguity caused by pretending that a word like *policeman* is generic, it is the assumption that sex is a relevant characteristic when referring to a person's profession, and that there is something "different" or inferior about women who are poets or men who are nurses.

(3) Terms which belittle.

These may overlap with the first category, as the belittling connotation of the term referring to women is often combined with a lack of parallel terminology.

INAPPROPRIATE	SUGGESTED ALTERNATIVES

a. Girls vs. women

Use of girl to refer to an adult female, especially a stranger	*woman*

We recognize that some adults refer to their friends as a group as *girls* or *boys* and find nothing belittling in such usage. However, in many contexts, the use of *girl* or *girls* for adults implies immaturity and relative unimportance. And the usage is not usually paralleled in references to men. Thus, *the girls in the office* work with *men*, seldom with *boys*. Such usage reflects an evaluation of the role of women as less important that that of men. A female Vice President would probably not be referred to as a *girl*, but a female clerk would most likely be a *girl*, while her male counterpart would be a *man*. The use of *boy* might reflect the person's extreme youth, or an attitude that people in lesser positions do not merit as much respect as their superiors. We suggest that this is as inappropriate as the sexist attitudes and that everyone would gain in dignity by the use of *men* and *women*.

INAPPROPRIATE	SUGGESTED ALTERNATIVES

b. Forms of address

honey, sweetie, dear, and similar terms to address women with whom one does not have a close relationship	No address form *or* person's name (when known) *or* generic term of address like *Ma'am* or *Sir* in contexts such as service encounters

(Of course when there is a close relationship between people, there is nothing wrong with reciprocal usage of terms of endearment.)

c. Derogatory labels

chick, broad, tomato, babe, and similar terms which treat women as sex objects or objects for consumption	neutral terms which treat people with dignity and respect

INAPPROPRIATE   SUGGESTED ALTERNATIVES

Expressions such as *Miss*
Fidditch to refer to the stereotypical fussy English teacher

(4) Use of adjectives, nouns, and other forms to reflect stereotypes

INAPPROPRIATE   SUGGESTED ALTERNATIVES

a. Associating characteristics with one sex only

masculine drive   drive
feminine wiles   wiles
feminine intuition   intuition

(The adjectives are unnecessary in the above examples.)

b. Using different adjectives to describe the same characteristic

outspoken man/bitchy
woman
prudent man/timid
or fearful woman

When used differentially to
describe the same trait, the
choice of adjectives reveals the
user's bias regarding the sexes.
Non-discriminatory usage requires
deciding on the appropriate
description regardless of sex,
and labelling both men and women
as either *prudent* or *fearful*,
for example.

c. Using different verbs to describe the same activity

men shout/
women scream/
men guffaw/
women giggle
men talk/
women chatter, gossip, etc.

The use of words often reveals
attitudes regarding the sexes. As
in the case of adjectives and nouns,
non-discriminatory usage, as well as
clarity, requires choosing the
appropriate term regardless of sex.
Thus, men may *giggle* and *gossip*,
etc.

*d. Using stereotyped adjectives and other descriptive expressions for one
sex only, such as including information regarding hair color or clothes
when referring to women, regardless of context*

The blond Ms. Rudnik is
Chief Executive Officer of
the firm.

Prime Minister Margaret
Thatcher, wearing a dark blue
suit, arrived for the meeting
of heads of government.

The adjectives are irrelevant here and would rarely be used in references to men. This is a reflection of our stereotyped beliefs regarding the importance of looks and dress for women in all situations. It is, of course, appropriate, in certain contexts, to refer to such characteristics for both women and men. Here, as elsewhere, it is a matter of treating the sexes equally.

Finally, equal treatment of the sexes involves remembering that women constitute approximately half of humanity. Language, both spoken and written, frequently renders women all but invisible. Lists of famous people consisting only of men, references exclusively in terms of "generic" *he* and *man*, and other types of common usage may create an image of an all-male world. This is reinforced by the fact that men have dominated many spheres of activity. One cannot, of course, include women in a list of presidents of the U.S.A. until a woman has held that office. But there is no reason for making women invisible in areas where they have been present, or for assuming that people in general, including hypothetical persons, are male.

The suggestions offered above are but a few of the alternatives available to those who wish to break with the traditional clichés and stereotypes and adopt non-sexist usage. You will find that English is indeed rich in resources for creating a usage which reflects sensitivity to the social implications of language. You will also discover that the practice of non-sexist usage is fully compatible with elegance, precision, and other criteria of good style.

A Selected List of Guidelines for Non-Sexist Usage

The list which follows includes a representative sample of publishers' guidelines, and selected material in other categories. In addition to material received directly from the publishers concerned, we have consulted a number of other sources, especially the earlier bibliography prepared by Blaubergs and Rieger.

Classifications used in the following list are: book publishers; professional and scholarly organizations; general, including the media, other groups, and handbooks and manuals designed for a general or specialized audience.

Book Publishers

Ginn and Company. Lexington, MA. *Treatment of Women and Minority Groups.* (2 pp). 1975.

_____. *Editorial and Graphic Criteria for Art and Design.* (5 pp).

Harper & Row, Publishers, Inc. NY. College Department. *Harper & Row Guidelines on Equal Treatment of the Sexes in Textbooks.* (5 pp). 1976.

Holt, Rhinehart & Winston. NY. *Guidelines for the Development of Elementary and Secondary Instructional Materials.* 1975.

_____. College Department. *The Treatment of Sex Roles and Minorities.* 1976.

Houghton Mifflin Company. Boston. *Eliminating Stereotypes.* School Division Guidelines. (42 pp). 1981. (revision of *Avoiding Stereotypes: Principles and Applications.* 1975.)

Richard D. Irwin, Inc. Homewood, IL. *Guidelines for Richard D. Irwin Authors and Copy Editors for Equal Treatment of Men and Women.* (No Date.)

Macmillan Publishing Company. NY. School Division. *Guidelines for Creating Positive Sexual and Racial Images in Educational Materials.* (96 pp). 1975.

McGraw-Hill Book Company. NY. *Guidelines for Equal Treatment of the Sexes in McGraw-Hill Book Company Publications.* (No Date). (also available as ERIC Document Reproduction Service No. ED 098 574; reprinted in *Elementary English* 52 (May 1975):725-733.)

Prentice-Hall. Englewood Cliffs, N.J. *Prentice-Hall Author's Guide*, 5th ed. 1975.

Random House. NY. *Guidelines for Multiethnic/Nonsexist Survey.* (28 pp). 1976.

Scott, Foresman and Company. Glenview, IL. *Guidelines for Improving the Image of Women in Textbooks.* (11 pp). 1972 and 1974.

South-Western Publishing Co. Cincinnati, OH. *Fair and Balanced Treatment of Minorities and Women.* 1976.

John Wiley & Sons. NY. College Editing Dept. *Wiley Guidelines on Sexism in Language.* (20 pp, unnumbered). 1977.

Professional Organizations

American Psychological Association, Task Force on Issues of Sexual Bias in Graduate Education. "Guidelines for Nonsexist Use of Language." *American Psychologist* 30 (1975): 682-684.

American Psychological Association. "Guidelines for Nonsexist Language in APA Journals." Publication Manual Change Sheet 2, *American Psychologist* 32 (1977): 487-494 (reprinted in *Educational Researcher* 7.3 (1978): 15-17.)

American Society for Public Administration, National Committee on Women in Public Administration. *The Right Word: Guidelines for Avoiding Sex-Biased Language*. Ed. E. Siedman. (8 pp, unnumbered). 1979.

American Sociological Association, Committee on the Status of Women in Sociology. "Sexist Biases in Sociological Research: Problems and Issues." *Footnotes* (Jan 1980). (reprinted by Project on the Status and Education of Women, Association of American Colleges, 1818 R Street, NW, Washington, DC 20009.) (Does not focus on language usage.)

International Association of Business Communicators. San Francisco. *Without Bias: A Guidebook for Non-discriminatory Communication*. Ed. J.E. Pickens, P.W. Rao, and L.C. Roberts. (77 pp). 1977.

National Council of Teachers of English. Urbana, IL. "Guidelines for Nonsexist Usage of Language in NCTE Publications." 1975. (reprinted in *Sexism and Language*. Ed. A.P. Nilsen, H. Bosmajian, H.L. Gershuny and J.P. Stanley. Urbana, IL: NCTE, 1977, 181-191.)

Teachers of English to Speakers of Other Languages. "TESOL Quarterly Style Sheet." *TESOL Quarterly* 13.4 (1979):606-611 (reprinted in 14.4 (1980): 543-548.)

General

American Press Women. "Guidelines to Eliminate Sexism in the Media." *Press Woman* 39.6 (1976).

Bank of America Communications Dept., Box 370000, San Francisco, CA 94137. *Guidelines for the Equal Treatment of All Employees in Bank of America Internal Communications*. 1975.

Burr, E., S. Dunn and N. Farquhar. *Guidelines for Equal Treatment of the Sexes in Social Studies Textbooks*. Los Angeles: Westside Women's Committee, P.O. Box 24D20, Los Angeles, CA 90024. 1973.

Chicago Women in Publishing, P.O. Box 11837, Chicago IL. *Equality in Print: A Guide for Editors and Publishers*. (23 pp). (No Date).

Hogan, P. "Sexism in the Corporate Press." *Journal of Organizational Communication* 2 (Winter 1973): 1-6.

Lutheran Church in America, Office of Communications. *Guidelines for Screening Bias for Writers and Editors.* (14 pp). 1974.

Miller, C. and K. Swift. *The Handbook of Nonsexist Writing for Writers, Editors and Speakers*, NY: Lippincott & Crowell, Publishers. (134 pp). 1980.

Newsday, 550 Stewart Ave., Garden City, Long Island, NY 11530. *Editorial Guidelines.* 1976.

Ontario Press Council, 151 Slater St., Suite 708, Ottawa, Ont. K1P 5H3. *Sexism and the Newspapers.* (26 pp). 1978.

Persing, B.S. *The Nonsexist Communicator.* East Elmhurst, NY: Communications Dynamics Press. (168 pp). 1978.

Swidler, L. "Linguistic Sexism." Editorial, *Journal of Ecumenical Studies* 2 (Spring 1974).

United Presbyterian Church in the U.S.A., Advisory Council on Discipleship and Worship, 475 Riverside Dr., Rm. 1020, N.Y., NY 10115. *The Power of Language among the People of God and the Language about God 'Opening the Door': A Resource Document.* (48 pp). 1979.

U.S. Department of Labor, Manpower Administration. "Job Title Revisions to Eliminate Sex-and-Age Referent Language from the Dictionary of Occupational Titles," 3rd ed. Washington D.C.: Government Printing Office. 1975.

Wendlinger, R.M. and C. Matthews. "How to Eliminate Sexist Language from your Organization's Writing: Some Guidelines for the Manager and Supervisor." In *Affirmative Action for Women: A Practical Guide.* Ed. D. Jongeward, D. Scott et al. Reading, MA: Addison-Wesley. 1973.

Women on Words and Images, Inc. *Sex Fairness in Education Division Communications, Products and Dissemination Strategies.* Washington, D.C.: National Advisory Council on Women's Educational Programs. 1977.

Bibliography

Blaubergs, M. and M. Rieger. "Guidelines for Non-Sexist Language: A Bibliography." Athens, Georgia: The University of Georgia, Institute for Behavioral Research. (mimeo) 1979.

Index